REST *for the* weary Mama

*Words of Hope and Encouragement
for the Worn-Out Mom*

Morgan A. Ellis

ENDORSEMENTS

Rest for the Weary Mama is a warm place for exhausted hearts and souls to land. Curl up with a cup of hot tea and a blanket and allow these words of hope to wrap you up in a gentle hug. Morgan's personal stories and heartfelt words will give you permission to be right where you are, and yet, offer simple, practical tools to grow more meaningful, satisfying lives. Her words gently point you back to the heart of the Father, reminding the reader that He is waiting to meet you in the messiness of motherhood.

Being a life coach, I read a lot of resources focused on personal growth. This book, hands down, is my new favorite "motherhood manual" to recommend for all moms in the trenches! What a relatable, practical, easy-to-read, breath of fresh air.

Courtney Lockridge
Life, leadership, and relationship coach

Rest for the Weary Mama is an amazingly encouraging, spiritually focused, uplifting, and practical book that will touch the heart of every weary mama. Morgan's honesty and transparency as she shares her personal story are not only captivating but also meaningful as she encourages moms to persevere through the daily, very real challenges of motherhood while maintaining a tender focus on who they are in the Lord. Blessings upon blessings are in store for all who journey through this wonderful book.

Patricia Wilkerson
Bible Study Fellowship International Teaching Leader

Published by hope*books
2217 Matthews Township Pkwy
Suite D302
Matthews, NC 28105
www.hopebooks.com

hope*books is a division of hope*media

Printed in the United States of America

First paperback edition.
Paperback ISBN: 979-8-89185-051-4
Hardcover ISBN: 979-8-89185-052-1
Ebook ISBN: 979-8-89185-053-8
Library of Congress Number: 2024931109

This book is dedicated to:

My amazing husband, the man of my dreams and the biggest supporter of me and our family. This dream would never have become a reality without your love, encouragement, and continuous support. Thank you for being my greatest sounding board and faithful companion in this parenting journey.

To my three beautiful children, Gabriel, Elijah, and Adelle. It is such an honor to be your mom and I treasure each of you with all my heart. I wouldn't be the woman I am today without you three keeping me on my toes and keeping me humble. Although our lives are messy and imperfect, I wouldn't want it any other way. Thank you for this gift of motherhood.

TABLE OF CONTENTS

INTRODUCTION

Doug Fields said, "If a person is breathing, they need encouragement."[1] I must say, I agree wholeheartedly, especially if you are a mom. The road of motherhood can feel very lonely and exhausting, filled with many discouraging moments. I believe we all could use some extra encouragement to stay the course and run the race set before us as mamas. Thank you for being here, taking a step of faith in reading this book, and allowing me to share a little bit of my story and some encouragement with you. I hope and pray that this book will bring you comfort in whatever season of motherhood you find yourself in and hope for the journey ahead. I have poured my heart into these pages with the goal that some mama, somewhere, who is feeling lonely, discouraged, or burnt out may find hope. There is healing and rest in the truth who God is and who you are in Him.

If your cup is empty today, I understand. I've been there far too many times. Unfortunately, I cannot fill your cup; only Jesus can do that. This book is me pouring out my cup, my heart, to you in hopes that the overflow of mine might point you to the only One who is capable of filling yours.

As women and mothers in a world full of distractions, it can be hard to find firm footing. We are pulled in a thousand different directions every day—not to mention the lack of adequate sleep for years! It can feel lonely, isolating, and discouraging trying to raise our babies in this chaotic world, all while trying to stay grounded. In this book, I will share stories from my own motherhood journey (so far), some of the ways I have found healing from my past, and how lies were infiltrating my mind as a mom. I will also share passages of scriptures that have been a lifeline to me in this parenting journey. My hope for you is that as you read the many words ahead you will find something here to bring you a renewed spirit and encouragement for the years ahead.

This is not a parenting book or a self-help book. Rather, this is a book filled with words and love from one mama in the trenches to another. This is a book for the mama who is tired, lonely, overworked, and perhaps feeling inadequate. This book is to encourage and build you up so that you can live your life and do this whole mothering thing with more confidence and joy—not on your own but leaning on the Perfect One.

As gold is purified and refined by fire, you and I are also purified and refined through the fires of parenting. Motherhood is the most humbling and life-giving job, but finding joy in the mundane seasons can be a challenge. Before becoming a mom, I never in a million years thought I would have to clean poop off walls or wrestle a toddler, into her car seat almost every day. Never did I think I would struggle with irritability and anger towards my children, but as a human being with limitations, I have found myself angry, bitter, and worn out many times, yelling and losing my temper over silly things. I only had a realistic picture of motherhood once I was knee-deep in it. I hope this book will speak the truth in a relatable and encouraging way.

A few years ago, on a much-needed retreat for rest, I found myself weeping on the bank of a river in Colorado. My heart was heavy with the burdens of life. I was in a downward spiral and didn't know how to get off the rollercoaster. As a mom of three young kids, ages eight, five, and three at the time, along with being a successful small business owner as a hairstylist, I was burned out with no work-life balance. I felt like I had been burning the candle at both ends for nearly a decade, building a business all while having three babies. I was depressed, anxious, and saw no light at the end of a very dark tunnel. Yet, I believe God brought me to that exact moment of stillness to stop me in my tracks. As I listened to the whispering breeze through the tall grass and felt the cool water rush over my bare feet, I felt a stirring in my soul. It was the loudest and clearest I had ever felt God's presence. I heard Him speaking to my heart (not audibly, but clearly nonetheless) that it was going to be okay, that He loved me, and to trust Him with the next steps. I breathed in the fresh mountain air and felt the Holy Spirit filling me in a new way with every breath. My heart had been so heavy for so long, but I felt a weight lifting. I knew I was being called to make a BIG change in my life, and God was giving me little breadcrumbs to follow along the way. If I wanted to experience the freedom and the true, extravagant life God had in store for me, I knew I would need to let go of what I thought my life should look like and lean into how God was leading me in new directions.

I left my weekend in Colorado transformed. I returned to my regular life but knew it was time to pivot. After much prayer and counsel, I decided it was time to leave my thriving, full-time job behind the salon chair and focus my entire energy on my family. My heart's deepest desire was to be a good mom and although I didn't feel like I was a bad one; something, somewhere along the way just got out of wack. Despite loving being a hairstylist, I was not prioritizing my time wisely and had let my job turn me into a shell of a person. It was time to make a change. I was fearful but ultimately choosing to follow God is never wrong. I decided to lean into His leading and listen to His whispers of guidance. It was not easy, but nothing worthwhile ever is.

My hope for you, dear one, is to finish the pages of this book feeling encouraged, seen, and more fully equipped to find true rest, even in the chaos of your daily life as a mom. May you close the pages of this book with a renewed identity in who you are as a daughter of the King of Kings, knowing you are worthy, beautiful, and uniquely created to be the mom God has made you to be. God personally and intricately designed you to be the mother of your children, and I believe with all my heart that you are capable of not just surviving the years ahead but thriving in them.

I invite you to grab a cup of coffee or tea and light a candle so we can chat, mama to mama. God has so much in store for you—I just know it!

For I know the plans I have for you," declares the LORD, "plans to prosper you and not to harm you, plans to give you hope and a future.
—JEREMIAH 29:11

PART I

MOTHERHOOD IS *HARD*

Being a mom is *hard*. It's not just carrying the baby and the delivery part. Not that bringing a baby into the world isn't freaking hard, because it is! And for many of us, it did not come easily. I have many friends and women I know who have gone through infertility or had major complications during their pregnancies and deliveries. Yet, the challenges we face during conception and delivery are just the tip of the iceberg when it comes to what lies ahead on the journey of motherhood. It is in the many days and years that follow having your baby where the true mothering takes place. It is in the daily

> *It is in the many days and years that follow having your baby where the true mothering takes place.*

tasks and often mundane routine where the real challenges can be found. Not every minute of every day is hard, but the truth is, raising good humans that will one day be worthwhile contributors to society is a lot of responsibility. That responsibility should never be taken lightly.

For far too many years in my motherhood journey, I had a sugar-coated perception of what this life would be like. I had idealistic views based on wholesome television programs I watched as a child and much of the advice from others didn't adequately seem to prepare me for the road ahead. I was weary in my season, feeling alone and isolated in my struggles. This was not because I didn't have support around me or friends to talk to, but because I didn't have someone who would look me in the eyes and say "I know. I've been there. I remember how hard this is. You are doing a good job. Hang in there. How can I help?" I am the type of person who has a really hard time asking for or accepting help from others, so I really just needed someone to come over and lend a hand without being asked. I know this is completely unrealistic, but how many of us could use a person like that in our corner? We could all use someone to show up without judgement or condemnation and help carry the load of life.

How many times did I wish to have a listening ear or an encouraging word at the beginning of my mothering years? Even now, I need that encouragement. These words are just as much for me as they are for you. Somehow, I made it through those little years, and even though my children are still quite young, I have a fresh perspective on how I want to portray motherhood to other mamas around me. I want to pull back the curtain, help build others up, and be authentic. I want to share the good, the bad, and the ugly so that others might feel a little less alone in their season of motherhood and find encouragement from someone else who is in the trenches right alongside you. I want to share my heart with you and cheer you on as you seek to do the hard work of raising those kiddos. And ultimately, I want to point you to the source of true rest, no matter how worn down and tired you are, which is Jesus.

So, whether you are pregnant with your first baby or have been a mom for years, I know you are tired. Mentally, physically, maybe even spiritually, because raising kids is a hard job. I pray you will feel seen and as read these words know you are not alone. Motherhood simultaneously is the hardest, most humbling, and most refining job you will ever have, while also being the most rewarding. I am not the woman I was before I had children, and I honestly would never want to be her again. I am a better woman because I am a mother. When you see your babes learn something new or accomplish something they have worked hard for, or when the fruit of your hard work and prayers can finally be seen, it makes every hard day and night worth it.

> I am a better woman because I am a mother.

Even knowing all the hard things I have walked through in my life and as a mom so far (and I know there will be plenty more), I would do it all again. The challenges and hard times have shaped me into the woman I am today. I have become stronger and more reliant on God through the difficulties. I know I can face whatever lies ahead because He has already carried me through so much. I wouldn't change any part of my story because it has brought me here, to this exact moment, sitting with you.

I pray this for you today, sweet mama: that you don't look at the journey ahead as daunting or dwell on past mistakes with shame or guilt. Rather, allow all the bumps along the way to shape you into the amazing mama God is creating you to be. Allow Him to work through every circumstance, every heartbreak, and every disappointment to mold you and create something beautiful in you. May you always remember to go to Him when you are worn down by life, finding rest in His loving embrace. May your life leave behind a beautiful legacy of faith and a true model of what it looks like to rest in Jesus, even in the storms of life.

CHAPTER ONE

BECOMING A MOM

*For this child I have prayed, and the Lord has
granted me the petition that I made to Him.*
—*1 Samuel 1:27*, ESV

Dreams vs. Reality

Becoming a mom was something that I had longed for since before I can remember. While my husband and I were still dating, we would occasionally talk about the future. We would dream about a family and what our lives might look like "one day." I sometimes worried, "What if I can't have children?" or "Will I be a good mother?" To us, having a family was something we both longed for as we dreamed about our future together, yet neither of us could have foreseen the journey God would bring us on to become parents and raise our children.

Dreaming about something and seeing it become a reality are two very different things. I knew I wanted to be a mom, but I didn't really know what that meant. After my husband and I had been married for a little while, the "baby fever" began to set in. I knew I wanted to be pregnant and feel life growing inside me. I wanted to share sweet snuggles with a newborn. I wanted to share beach days, push little ones on the swing at the park, and go on grand adventures as a family. Many dreams swirled around in my mind of what it meant to be a mom, what that would look like, and how I would mother my children. Yet all those dreams came crashing down in the aftermath of my firstborn. I was not physically, mentally, or spiritually prepared for what lay ahead in my day-to-day life as a mom.

As a first-time mom, going through labor and delivery was life-altering. No amount of books or classes could have truly prepared me for the experience. It was longer and more arduous than I had anticipated—the most challenging thing I had ever done. And as it often goes, it looked nothing like the birth plan I so innocently prepared. And yet, I would do it all again in a heartbeat because it gave me my sweet son. I somehow think back on the day he was born fondly even though the reality was we both could have died. I think most of us moms can agree, even the ones who have experienced the worst trauma in their birth experiences—and I know quite a few of you who have—we would do it all again if it were the only way to receive our kids. God genuinely brings beauty from ashes.

Without much time to process what had just happened to me physically, my husband and I were packed up and sent on our way to our new life as Mom and Dad. It was all quite a whirlwind. I don't know about you, but as I crossed the threshold of our home for the first time carrying our new little babe, my heart began to panic about everything. Thoughts and doubts consumed my mind almost immediately. I had no clue what I was doing. However, I never wanted to let anyone in on that little, secret part of my heart, so I wrapped it up tight and pushed the doubts down deep. To those around me, I was calm and seemed to naturally jump right into motherhood. Yet, on the inside doubts and fears swirled. Over time, putting on that brave face slowly chipped away at who I thought I was.

I was still in cosmetology school when my first son was born. My maternity leave was six short weeks. This was barely enough time to recover from my third-degree tear and figure out how to do all the baby things for the first time. After graduation I went straight to work building my business while still in the throws of mothering. We got into a groove and 2 years later, baby number two came along. Although my second son's birth was much easier on my body, and I recovered more quickly than the first time around, I fell to different pressures and decided to go back to work far too quickly after he was born – only two short weeks.

I didn't realize it at first, but after some time, I began to understand I was suffering from postpartum depression. I would cry for hours and be completely unmotivated to do anything on my days off. I felt desperately alone and wildly underqualified in every area. Some nights, I would wake up for a middle-of-the-night feeding and decide to stay awake, hoping to catch a few moments of alone time before someone needed me again. Yet, inevitably, either the baby wouldn't go back to sleep, or my older son would wake up for some reason. I was madly exhausted and in desperate need of rest – whatever that meant. Although the early years are a bit of a blur on the timeline of my life, it was through the darkness and in the desperation that God started to pull me up and out of my pit of despair. He began to slowly point me back towards the light and remind me where my true strength and refuge would be found; in Him.

He reached down from on high and took hold of me; he drew me out of deep waters. He rescued me from my powerful enemy, from my foes, who were too strong for me.
—2 SAMUEL 22:17–18

A couple of years later, baby number three joined our ranks with spirit and vigor in the birth of our first daughter. Although I tried to give myself more time before heading back to work this time around, another season of depression hit as I transitioned and adjusted to being a mom of three. It was the start of a downward trajectory for me, both spiritually and emotionally. I slowly became more and more distant from the woman I used to be. Busier than ever before, I lost sight of what was truly important.

As most of us can attest, our big dreams of becoming moms and starting a family differ greatly from our realities. All our births are different, whether you come to be a mom like me through the traditional route, whether you adopt, or whether you need fertility treatments. Our stories of becoming moms are as unique as our children themselves. We can know we are truly blessed and still feel weary because motherhood is exhausting. I had been blessed beyond my wildest dreams

> We can know we are truly blessed and still feel weary because motherhood is exhausting.

with three healthy children and a loving husband, yet the reality of working full-time, raising three babies, being a loving and devoted wife, and everything in between was a lot to handle. I found myself buckling under the pressure, and little pieces of my heart seemed to slowly fade into darkness over the first few years of being a mom.

If you find yourself in a similar season of motherhood—feeling lonely, exhausted, and just trying to make it through the day—I beg you, coming from a mom who didn't go through it very gracefully, don't let these years be stolen from you by cultural pressures or even your own pressures. We tend to think we have to do it all and be it all, but you don't. As cliché as it may sound, soak up every second of these little years because once they're gone, you can't get them back. If you are not feeling like yourself, find someone to talk to. Give yourself a lot of grace while you are learning to do this whole mothering thing. Motherhood will some days bring you to the brink of desperation, but it is typically in those places where God meets us tenderly and personally. His ultimate rest is sometimes found in the deepest, darkest places of our souls.

Lean in to where God is meeting you today and in this season. Because I believe fully that He does not desire for you to just survive in this season, but He is equipping you to thrive—to live your life, even the exhausting years of motherhood, with abundance, joy, and even, dare I say, rest.

How God Defines a Mom

The marble not yet carved can hold the form
of every thought the greatest artist has. [2]
—Michelangelo

"Mother," as defined in the Hebrew language literally translates to "strong water." The symbols, created by an ox and waves, literally representing strength and life. *Eym, Ima,* Mother.[3] We each have been made in God's image; thus, we are each a beautiful, unique representation of our Creator. We as mothers have the beautiful privilege to represent our Creator God's character in strength, life, wisdom, nurture, protection, home, and so much more. *Mother* is all-encompassing. Do you believe that today?

I love hearing stories of moms who can lift some ridiculously heavy object off a trapped child. Moms will go to extreme lengths to protect their babies, but it's more than that. We protect while we nurture. We show strength while we care. What a God we have who loves us in this same way.

Woven throughout scripture, God whispers the truth that a godly mother and woman is humble, kind, generous, patient, speaks with wisdom, and yet holds her tongue. She trusts and fears the Lord, is hard-working, has a cheerful spirit, and has a servant's heart. He reminds her not to be afraid or anxious but rather to come to Him with her burdens and cares and to cast them at His feet. She is redeemed, loved, cherished, adored, delighted in, and beloved. When we walk closely with our Creator, He shapes us into who He wants us to be. As we are sanctified (just a fancy, churchy word meaning we are being made more like Jesus) through the Holy Spirit, we, too, can exemplify these beautiful qualities in our daily lives. It is a long, slow process, but it is attainable—just not on our own. It takes trusting our lives in God's hands so that He can mold us into this type of woman.

Like a sculptor who slowly chisels away at a larger piece of stone and creates a beautiful sculpture that only he can picture in his mind, so it is with God. Only He knows what He wants to create in you and your life. Contrary to the earthy sculptor, God is sweet to give us a glimpse into what He is creating. He chisels away slowly at our exteriors, our selfishness, pride, bitterness, envy, impatience, and hot-headedness. He smooths out the rough edges and carves into our hearts those beautiful qualities He desires for us. He is kind, generous, humble, hard-working, faithful, patient, and wise. The further He gets into His work, the more we exemplify His character and resemble the women and mother He longs for us to be.

> The Creator who spoke the universe into existence, who placed every star in the heavens, personally and intimately, is shaping you into something more beautiful than you could ever imagine.

It changes everything when you allow the truth of who God says you are to override who you think you are. You may think you are just a hunk of stone, of no use to anyone, no good for anything, but God knows otherwise. He sees the beautiful sculpture underneath. The Creator who spoke the universe into existence, who placed every star in the heavens, personally and intimately, is shaping you into something more beautiful than you could ever imagine. When you let that sink in, you can't help but live your life in a way that is pleasing to Him. You may not feel adequate or equipped to raise those babies, but God designed and chose you specifically to be the mother of your children. He is faithful to equip you for the task.

Being a "good mom" isn't the goal.

Being a "good mom" isn't the goal. Instead, let's make being a "holy mom" our goal—a mom who first and foremost loves and trusts God with all her heart. She leans into her insufficiencies and allows Jesus to fill in the gaps where she inevitably falls short. "The Wife of Noble Character," described in Proverbs 31:10–31, paints a beautiful (albeit a bit intimidating) picture of what a "holy mom" might look like.

> *She is clothed with strength and dignity;*
> *she can laugh at the days to come.*
> *She speaks with wisdom, and faithful instruction is on her tongue.*
> PROVERBS 31:25-26

It can feel defeating to read about this idealistic woman and compare yourself to everything she does. She seems perfect. She does it all. She is admired by all those around her, including her children and husband. How can we ever measure up to these standards? I don't think God inspired Solomon to write these words to make you or me feel insufficient or inadequate. Rather, I believe God uses the woman in Proverbs 31 as a beautiful example of who He can shape us into as we trust more in Him as the provider, the sustainer, and the giver of all things. The writer goes on to say that "charm is deceptive, and beauty is fleeting, but a woman who fears the Lord is to be praised" (Prov. 31:30). I believe this to be the whole purpose of this passage: to remind us, especially as moms, to lean into who God is and to trust Him completely. A holy mom is one who binds her family together and humbly admits she can't do it all while wholeheartedly relying on the One who can.

In our humanity, we will always fall short. Our waters may run dry when we try to sustain them on our own. Yet, Jesus reminds us, just like the woman at the well in John 7:38, "Whoever believes in me, as scripture has said, rivers of living water will flow from within them." Jesus is our living water. When we come to Him and stay connected to Him as our source, our waters will never run dry. Does your cup feel empty today, mama? I've been there too—many times. Forgetting to connect or reconnect my heart to the true source is what leaves me feeling dry. Find space today to sit in the presence of your Holy Creator. Allow Him to fill you up in the way only He can.

Rejoice always, pray continually, give thanks in all circumstances; for this is God's will for you in Christ Jesus.
—*1 Thessalonians 5:16–18*

God provides us with all the tools we need to be exceptional mamas; we just need to remember to use them. The most powerful tool you have at your disposal is prayer. I met a lovely woman a few years ago at a consignment shop. Her kids were grown, and we started chit-chatting about parenting and motherhood while we stood in the checkout line. Her words impacted me, and I have carried them with me ever since. She said, "The only way I survived motherhood was on my knees." She went on to say that she still prays for and over her children daily, even though they are grown. What an amazing example of what it looks like to be a godly, "holy mom," a real-life Proverbs 31 woman. I'm sure there were many times when she messed up or made mistakes with her kids, but she knew where to go when things got tough. She knew, and we can also know, that God cares deeply for us and wants us to come to Him with all we're going through. When we know Jesus and have the Holy Spirit, we have the power of our Creator living inside us. That power is the only way to truly meet our God-given potential as mamas. Without it, we leave out a critical piece of the puzzle and we will never feel complete.

There is power in prayer and posturing your heart towards your Creator in gratitude and humility. Luke writes in Luke 5:16, "Jesus often withdrew to lonely places and prayed." Jesus continuously sought refuge in the presence of His Father for strength and stamina to stay the course that was set before Him. Jesus was not surprised by any of the things

> *There is power in prayer and posturing your heart towards your Creator in gratitude and humility.*

He faced during His time on Earth, but, being fully human, He still knew the importance of constantly checking in and regaining His strength from the Father. If you feel drained, isolated, weary, or ready to throw in the towel, don't let that create distance between you and God. Instead, let it be the reason you run to Him and seek His counsel. He has been there. He knows what you are feeling and what you are facing, and He is the only One who can strengthen you when you feel weak.

We can learn much from Jesus' example of the importance of seeking intentional time in prayer with the Father. We learn to seek rest at His feet when we feel we can't go another step or when we feel burdened by the heaviness of life. Although we will never do it perfectly, we can take strides every day toward being the women and moms God created us to be. God says that you are loved beyond measure (Rom. 5:8), chosen (John 15:16), fearfully and wonderfully made (Ps. 139:13–14), called to clothe yourself in compassion, kindness, humility, gentleness, and patience (Col. 3:12), to live in peace and be thankful (Col. 3:15), and most importantly, to fear the Lord (Ps. 34:9; Prov. 31:30) knowing He is the only place to gather true strength, hope, peace, and rest.

Comparison Trap

I have a nasty habit of scrolling social media and then feeling pretty bad about myself after the fact. I gaze upon women (mostly strangers) who are prettier, have a nicer house, have kids who look more put together, their lives look picture-perfect, and somehow forget that most of the time it's just an act. I compare myself to a seemingly impossible standard and it leaves me feeling depleted before the day even begins. Have you been there too? As we learn to embrace who God has made us to be, it can be easy to start comparing ourselves to others. It is a natural trap we all find ourselves in at one point or another. So, if you are struggling this way, know you are in good company. Looking to the left or right and admiring the strengths and gifts of other mamas where we ourselves fall short is a natural temptation, but it isn't healthy. It is said that comparison is the thief of joy. If you continue to compare yourself to others, you will inevitably have the joy stolen right out of your season of motherhood.

Not only does comparing ourselves to others steal the joy of our own accomplishments and successes, but it also turns into a breeding ground for bitterness and lack of contentment. In these places, we disregard who God has made us to be and fail to own who we are along with our unique season and situation. I want to remind you and myself that you were not made to be anyone but exactly who you are. God gave you distinct gifts and callings that are just for you. Don't let comparison squander the joy waiting for you in this season of your life. Stop looking to the left and the right. Stop comparing who God made someone else to be without stopping to celebrate and recognize the amazing woman and mom He made *you* to be. You are just who God created you to be, and you are the mom He chose to raise the children in your care. When you live in a constant state of discontentment, you overlook the blessings God has specifically given to you. When you are focused on others around you, you reject the beautiful life God has given to you.

You were not made to be anyone but exactly who you are.

Have you ever celebrated how God uniquely made you? Have you ever taken the time to genuinely thank God for making you the way He did? It's so easy to celebrate others, but when it comes to finding strengths in ourselves, it seems so uncomfortable. If you can relate, I'm right there with you. It feels self-glorifying to recognize your own strengths, but this couldn't be further from the truth. God gave each of us different strengths, gifts, and abilities that uniquely make us who we are. A common thread runs through each of us as moms, but ultimately, we each get to bring something different to the table. We are each remarkable and distinct, representing different parts of our Creator. Take a moment today to write out some of your unique strengths. If this is hard, ask someone close to you to point out some strengths they see in you, especially regarding motherhood. You may be surprised by what someone else sees in you that you don't see in yourself.

When I was a new mom of two, getting out of the house seemed to be the biggest feat of the week, not only because of all the things I needed to pack just to make a "quick" trip anywhere, but also because of the daunting fear that loomed in the back of my head of how to handle a newborn and a newly potty-trained toddler should some sort of bathroom issue arise. If you have been there, you know what I mean. Any newly potty-trained kiddo requires seemingly no less than 1,000 visits to the restroom, easily turning your thirty-minute grocery run into an hour or more.

I recall a situation from these early years with my two sons that really challenged me as a mom, especially in comparing myself to others. It was supposed to be a typical grocery store run. Get in, get out. Nothing fancy to prepare for, just the usual haul. I was relatively new to this whole two-kid game, and so, of course, this simple errand already felt dreadful even before it began. We made it into the store, took our first potty break, and were on our way. With a little pep talk, I bribed my toddler to be well-behaved with a free cookie from the bakery at the end of our shopping. Everything seemed to be going smoothly, and I was feeling pretty good about the whole experience. As we finished putting our last items in the cart, I was so proud to be able to push our cart over to the bakery to get my son his well-deserved cookie. Praying the cookie would buy me a few more minutes of good behavior at the checkout counter, I wasn't ready for what came next.

My son, feeling very confident and happy about his choice of a rainbow sprinkle cookie, took one bite and proceeded to throw the biggest fit ever, including throwing the confection onto the floor, wanting to change his selection to the chocolate chip cookie instead—buyer's remorse in toddler form. Not having a cookie set him off into an extreme reaction and an intense end to our grocery run. Here I was, newborn baby sweetly sleeping in his car seat in the cart, placing items on the conveyor belt, and restraining my toddler like a mental patient trying to prevent him from bolting back to the bakery. I felt the eyes of fellow shoppers piercing me like daggers, leaving me wanting to crawl into a hole and die. I'm proud to say that although I was mortified by the whole situation, I stood my ground, and he ended up with no cookie at the end of it all. I wish I could say we got out of the store and that was the end of that, but no. The saga continued when we got to the car. I set my son down to load up the groceries. Faster than lightning, that kid dashed back into the store and up the escalator. I stood in disbelief, frozen in place, not knowing if I should run after him. I couldn't leave my newborn to follow him, and the sweet bagger (no older than sixteen) who had helped me out to the car stood there petrified, not knowing what to do either. The poor kid was probably traumatized by all this, too. Not knowing what else to do, we put the groceries away as quickly as possible and sprinted back into the store to find the escapee. Halfway up the escalator, newborn in tow, I saw the bakery employee coming down the other side with my older son beside her. At this point, it took everything in me not to burst into hysterical tears. I collected my son, made it to the car at last, strapped him in his car seat, and just sat there for no less than five minutes, staring forward in silence and disbelief. This moment defined me as a mom for a long time, because I felt isolated.

I questioned whether I was the only one with a child who acted like this. I contemplated all the things I did wrong. I wondered if the poor checkout kid thought, *Well, this mom has no clue what she is doing.* I began to doubt myself and avoid hard situations out of fear of failing again. This was when comparison began to creep in and weave its nasty little web of lies all around my thoughts. I had never seen any other kid act this way, so I felt alone. I know full well now, after being in this parenting game for much longer, that there are many other kids and moms who go through similar situations. When you go through something like this, it is hard to remove the feeling of guilt, but sometimes it isn't your fault. Sometimes kids are just kids, testing their boundaries and running amok. It doesn't mean we let them get away with it, but it does mean we let go of the shame, guilt, and embarrassment we carry with us from these situations.

Reflecting on that moment, I don't think I could have done much differently. I did my best in a situation I had no experience handling. The only thing I wish I could change was the grace I withheld from myself and the fear I carried for years afterward, worried every time I went somewhere with the kids that something like this would happen again. I also wish I could change the years spent thinking I was alone, the only one struggling. I have experienced many other extreme moments just like this over the years. The difference is that now I understand I'm not the only one struggling. Even if many people don't understand or have compassion, I am not alone, and neither are you. Maybe you have been there before. Maybe you have been on the opposite end, judging the poor mama trying to handle her unhinged child. Have you ever thought, *Thank goodness my kid isn't acting like that?* Comparison breeds one of two outcomes: insecurity or pride.

Comparison breeds one of two outcomes: insecurity or pride.

Comparing myself and my kids to others has, at times, created an unnecessary weight I've carried into other areas of my parenting. Not only has it stolen my joy, but also my confidence in my ability to mother my children well. I have taken the weight of any hard moment as a sign I was doing something wrong, when in truth, most often, I am just dealing with normal childlike behaviors. No one likes to talk about the hard things they face with their kids. Everyone tends to put their best foot forward and hide their real lives from the public eye. It isn't my favorite thing to talk about either, but if no one ever talks about the hard stuff, we end up with a false narrative that we are the only ones struggling. Satan would like nothing more than to isolate you in your trials—to cut you off from others who are there to support you.

The truth is that there are no kids who are good all the time. There has never been a parent in history to escape dealing with some sort of meltdown or tantrum at some point. We must stop telling ourselves false narratives that we are the only ones struggling or dealing with challenging things as parents. We must stop comparing our lives and our kids to others. Just as you have been created uniquely and have been given distinct gifts from your Creator, so have your children. Comparison can lead to two outcomes: insecurity or pride—two sides of the same coin. Insecurity focuses on what you can't do or don't have (forgetting what God can and has given you), while pride focuses on what you can do or do have (forgetting God altogether). Both will rob you of true joy and peace.

Where do you tend to compare yourself to others? Is it like me, with your children? Is it in wishing you had a nicer home? Maybe you compare your vacations to someone else's. Maybe you compare what you do for your kids' birthdays to the other moms and families at school. Whatever it is, we all have something, somewhere we find ourselves comparing and envying others. And although it is normal to do so, it is like a disease that will take over your heart leading to a life of discontentment and bitterness.

A heart at peace gives life to the body, but envy rots the bones
—PROVERBS 14:30

King Solomon said it well when he wrote this proverb, reminding us that envy—just another word for comparison—will rot you from the inside out. It steals your joy and spoils the good that God has already given you. So, how do we combat envy? How do we avoid this very dangerous trap that the world so easily sets for us around every corner? The opposite of envy is contentment, and the opposite of comparison is confidence. This is not prideful confidence, but humble assurance in God's plan for your life and gratitude for the blessings already bestowed on you. Now, I'm not saying this will be easy. It could very well be a lifelong struggle to overcome these feelings. Still, I believe the more intentional you are in practicing gratitude in your daily life for the family that you have and the children who are already yours, the easier it is to release comparing yourself to others and to fully trust in your heart, not just your head, that God has chosen this life specifically for you.

I tend to feel like a failure whenever my life feels messy or out of control. In my flesh, I feel judged, whether I am or not, and I take full responsibility for my children's actions as if they were my own. Instead of handling outbursts of childlike behavior calmly and rationally, I feel embarrassed and allow myself to be triggered into having my own mommy meltdown. It is easier to allow our emotions to run the show. It is easier to permit feelings of jealousy, discontentment, and bitterness in our hearts. It is more work to practice gratitude. It is harder to walk through the struggles of daily life and thank God for them anyway. But this is how you combat the lies of comparison: with truth and gratitude.

> *It is harder to walk through the struggles of daily life and thank God for them anyway.*

Whenever I share a recent parenting struggle on social media, floods of messages from other moms come in thanking me for sharing. Of course, I always get a few judgmental ones, but more often than not, other mamas thank me for sharing the real parts of parenting, including the hard things. We have all been tricked into thinking those around us don't struggle or that their kids have it all together. Social media paints a pretty picture, but it isn't the whole snapshot. The reality is that everyone has struggled at some point or another. Everyone probably has dirty dishes in their sink and laundry on the end of their beds. Everyone has walked through difficult things, even if they don't talk about it. Do not doubt God's goodness or faithfulness because you are caught up comparing your life to someone else's. Do not let envy or comparison rob you of the joy that is waiting for you, even if you are in a hard season.

God has blessed each of us specifically and uniquely. I struggle in many ways that you may not, and vice versa, and this is also true of ways God has chosen to bless me and my family in different ways than yours. To stop the temptation of envy and comparison, start by focusing on how God has specifically blessed you and thank Him today. When you keep your eyes and heart focused on how God is blessing you, even in the simplest things, you will find yourself too preoccupied to care about anyone else. Take a moment to find three things in your life you can be thankful for. If you can't think of three, start with one, and then ask God to open your eyes to others.

It is Satan's goal to keep us in the comparison trap. He knows exactly where we are vulnerable, and there is nothing off limits for him—even our children. The Bible reminds us in 1 Peter 5:18 to "be alert and of sober mind. Your enemy the devil prowls around like a roaring lion looking for someone to devour." So, when you feel discontentment or envy creeping in, remember those are not from God. God wants you to find contentment, joy, peace, and rest, while the enemy will keep you stuck in comparison and discontentment; while you toil and strive for things not meant for you. God has designed you and chosen you to be the mother of your children, and He does not make mistakes. Each brushstroke God makes in your life and in the world is intentional; only He, the artist, knows the purpose. Envy rots the bones, but gratitude strengthens our faith and allows us to experience God's desired peace and rest.

Let your eyes look straight ahead; fix your gaze directly before you.
—Proverbs 4:25

Keep your eyes fixed on Jesus, and all the things of this world will grow strangely dim. Do not compare your motherhood journey to the woman next to you, or to your own mother or grandmother, or to the neighbor down the street, or the other moms in the nursery at church. God is writing a unique story for each of us. There will be much turbulence along the way, but when you keep your gaze on the blessings right in front of you, you will find new purpose and strength, and ultimately find a deep lasting joy in your own motherhood journey.

We have each been given unique abilities, talents, and gifts that make us who we are. Paul writes in 1 Corinthians 12:14 that "the body is not made up of one part but of many." He reminds us that the foot does not think it is useless because it is not a hand, nor an ear because it is not an eye. Just like each of the unique and individual parts of our body have a role to play in keeping us alive, you also have a unique and individual purpose in the story of your family and of humanity. You were created for such a time as this, and no matter what your friends, coworkers, or even complete strangers on the internet are doing, this does not devalue you or what you are doing. Do not let comparison keep you from delighting in the life that God has given specifically to you. You can rest today and stop your toiling and equating yourself to others. Lean into who God has made *you*. God has called you to come to Him when you feel weary, burdened, and inadequate. As a result, He promises to give you rest—rest from needing to do it all and be it all, rest that seeks acclamation from Him, your Heavenly Father, instead of the superficial world around you. And that is enough.

Questions to Ponder

- ♥ What were some ways becoming a mom for the first time left you feeling blindsided?
- ♥ If you could talk to your younger mom self, what is one piece of advice you would give her?
- ♥ Read Proverbs 31. What stands out to you most about the woman described in this passage? Where are you challenged by most?

♥ Has there ever been a time or a season when you have compared yourself as a mom to someone else in your circle or even a stranger? What was it about this person that made you feel lesser than?

♥ How has God specifically blessed you? If you can't think of any, ask someone who knows you well to point some out to you. Remind yourself of these blessings every time you feel comparison starting to creep in.

Try This

Write down how God sees you from different passages of scripture and hang them up somewhere you can see them. Remind yourself just how treasured you are in God's eyes and that your identity is in Him. Here are some of my favorites you can start with, but feel free to find more:

Jeremiah	31:3
Psalm	139:14
Ephesians	2:10
Romans	8:13-17
1 Peter	2:9

CHAPTER TWO:

LONG DAYS
AND LONGER NIGHTS

God is our refuge and strength, an ever-present help in trouble.
Therefore we will not fear, though the earth give way and the mountains
fall into the heart of the sea, though its waters roar and foam and the
mountains quake with their surging. There is a river whose streams
make glad the city of God, the holy place where the Most High dwells.
God is within her, she will not fall; God will help her at break of day.
Psalm 46:1-5

I was so excited when I was pregnant with our first son, Gabriel, inching closer to his birth. He was a week past his due date, so I was more than ready for him to be born. I was anxious to hold him and to officially be a mom. Little did I know that Gabe would propel my husband and me into parenthood like a rocket. His birth was less than ideal, and he was a tough baby from day one. I loved him more than life itself, but man, I entered motherhood completely unprepared for the task.

Although I had spent months reading about birth, attending classes offered at the hospital, and doing my best to prepare for this moment, nothing can truly prepare you for your own unique birth experience. Some births are lovely and quick, others excruciating and drawn out. I've had three babies, and their births were all completely different and unique. I have talked to hundreds of women about their birth stories over the years, and not one has ever been the same. It is a personal and unique experience that no number of classes or books can truly prepare you for. They are fantastic tools, don't get me wrong, but I wish they came with a disclaimer at the beginning to let us all know, "Hey! Just a heads up: what you are going to experience will probably be nothing like this, but we hope this helps."

I suspect if you are reading this book, you have probably already gone through your own birth experience, and I'm sure I don't need to tell you that there is no one-size-fits-all when it comes to birth. The same is true of mothering. This is why we need each other. Maybe becoming a mom would be less scary if we had more open, honest discussions with those around us. Maybe we should approach motherhood with a little more compassion and understanding, knowing these sweet (most of the time) kiddos whom we love so much are also the reason we crack some days. Enter Jesus and grace—the two most important things we need as mamas.

Although the days are long and the nights can feel even longer, the years truly are short. In the words of the famous country singer Darius Rucker, "It won't be like this for long."[4] Don't let these years pass you by without soaking up every blessing God has for you in the midst of them, even the hard ones. There can be things pulling you in a million different directions, but remember, the most important job you have in this season is raising those babies (even if they aren't babies anymore). Some may say to put yourself first and make sure you don't lose yourself in motherhood. This may be true to a degree, but I would like to propose a different perspective. Put God first and see how the rest falls into place. You will find that when you truly put God first in your heart, there is more than enough love, time, and energy to go around—not just for your kids, but for your spouse and for yourself. On the flip side of not losing yourself in motherhood, I challenge you to find yourself in motherhood. There is so much joy and beauty to be found in motherhood, and God has more waiting in store for you along this journey. It is in the trusting, the waiting, and the daily grind that could quite possibly be the most difficult parts of motherhood, yet you can find rest at the feet of the Father even in the midst of long days and longer nights.

> *You will find that when you truly put God first in your heart, there is more than enough love, time, and energy to go around*

Flip The Script

After our first son was born, I could barely sit down for weeks following his delivery, and not just because of the third-degree tear. He was a restless babe, so our nights were tough. He was up every two to three hours for the first four months and still didn't sleep through the night until about nine months. The days were long and the nights even longer as a new mom already running on fumes. I remember being so tired I thought I would die. I was delirious some nights from exhaustion, but somehow, we made it through to the other side. If this is the season of motherhood you are in, I see you, mama. I know those nights are so long, and all the days can seem to run together. You've got this! You will get through it. Trust that this is just a season and that you will sleep again one day.

God promises to carry us through our storms—not that He will always calm them or make things easier, but He does promise to be with us through them. His promise in Deuteronomy 31:8 is that He never leaves us nor forsakes us. Even though it may feel like you are never going to sleep or feel like yourself again in the newborn season, I want to encourage you to hold on to the hope and truth that you will get through this season—faster than you think.

I recently learned that flamingos can lose some of their color after having babies. Their brilliant pink feathers fade to dull and white for a season while they are raising their young. The mama flamingo's color drains as they feed their babies because the nutrients typically used to make their feathers radiate are given to their young. However, the mama flamingos eventually regain their cheerful complexion as their chicks become more independent and eat independently. You, mama, amid long days and nights, may feel you have lost your sparkle. You may feel drained by the gradual and continual need to be needed all day, every day. Hang tight, friend! That pink will come back!

In Mark Batterson's book, *Win the Day*, he writes, "Everything we experience is a two-sided coin. It can either make us or break us."[5] His concept of flipping the script has really helped me, especially when I am in a state of desperation in parenting. Taking a hard moment and asking myself and, more importantly, God, *How can You use this? What can You teach me through this?* is how I have gotten through some of my most challenging seasons of parenting so far. It is how I have found great purpose even in the tough times.

And we know that in all things God works for the good of those who love him, who have been called according to his purposes.
—ROMANS 8:28

This verse is often quoted, and one common interpretation is that "all things happen for a reason." But what I hear in this verse, and believe to be true, is that not all things we walk through will be good or feel good. However, when we give all things to God—even the yucky, unpleasant, despicable things we walk through—He can use them for *His* good. If we allow Him, He won't let our pain and suffering be for nothing. He can use it for His glory, to help or encourage others around us walking through similar pains, and to help shape and refine our characters to be more like Him. God did not promise a smooth or painless life. On the contrary, Jesus Himself said, "In this world you will have trouble. But take heart! I have overcome the world" (John 16:33). There is a promise attached to the trouble for those who give their hardships over to God: we can trust that God is working in it and through it for our good and His purposes.

Feeling alone in your struggles may be one of Satan's biggest tricks on humanity. We tend to isolate ourselves when we feel like no one else understands or cares. It can suck the joy right out of what is supposed to be a beautiful part of life, leaving us exhausted. It is imperative to flip the script in your head that may tell you that you are alone, no one cares, or that you aren't good enough. Mama, God is equipping you for this job of motherhood. Every challenge you face is

> *Every challenge you face is an opportunity for Him to show up and show off.*

an opportunity for Him to show up and show off. When you feel you aren't enough, remember God is. When you feel you are alone, God is with you. When you feel no one cares, remember Jesus died for you, and He cares about you and everything you face. Remember these truths when your mind starts to turn on you.

We take captive every thought to make it obedient to Christ.
—2 CORINTHIANS 10:5

Taking your thoughts captive is the first step to flipping the script in your mind. A study by Queen's University says, "The average person has about 6,200 thoughts per day."[6] That is more than 258 thoughts per hour and at least four per minute. I'd go out on a limb and say most of us moms probably have more thoughts, but whether or not that is true, we are all doing a lot of thinking; there's a lot of

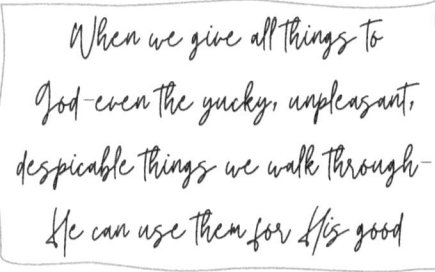

When we give all things to God—even the yucky, unpleasant, despicable things we walk through—He can use them for His good

power running through our minds at all times. Your thought life is the number one battleground for finding joy, seeking peace, and, ultimately, finding rest—especially in the chaotic, sometimes overwhelming season of motherhood. When we learn to talk to ourselves rather than listen to the false narratives played out in our heads, we can change our brain waves and thought patterns.

I still struggle daily with negative thoughts. It is why I love to journal and why I find it important to stay grounded in God's word. I am so thankful for a husband and good friends who help point me back to the truth when I start believing the lies. If you struggle with negative thoughts, try writing them down. There is something about writing these thoughts down and reading them out loud that helps expose the lies for what they are. Also, write down positive thoughts and truth. Find scripture that is empowering and encouraging. Say them out loud to yourself every day. Ruminate on the positive and watch your brain and thought life transform.

God is with you. God is for you. God is working. These are just a few of the simple truths I hang on to when life feels dark or heavy—when the nights feel so long or when I feel like I might break. "Come to me all who are weary and burdened, and I will give you rest" (Matt. 11:28). What Satan means to harm you, God can use for good. The most glorious sunrises come after the darkest nights. Trust God and let Him give you rest, knowing the morning is coming.

Morning is Coming

Because of the Lord's great love we are not consumed,
for his compassions never fail. They are new
every morning; great is your faithfulness.
—LAMENTATIONS 3:22–23

Watching the sunrise is one of my absolute favorite things to do. Every morning, if I am up before the sun, I crack the blinds in my living room and watch the sky change colors as the sun climbs higher. It is especially one of my favorite things to do on vacation. With every new place I travel, I make it a point to get up before dawn and watch the sunrise in that location. Watching the sunrise is a magic felt in the soul. I will never tire of seeing God's new masterpiece each morning. Each is a fresh reminder of His faithfulness, creativity, and majesty. The sky truly does proclaim the work of His hands (Ps. 19:1).

I have walked through many painful, dark seasons in parenting and life so far—darkness that has felt like it would never end and that I thought would swallow me up, and challenges that seemed far beyond my capacity. Yet here I stand—still in the midst of some challenges, while others are mere memories. God has walked with me every step of the way through every season. He has never abandoned me or left me to my own devices. Whenever I feel like I will never get out and the darkness overwhelms me, He gently reminds me to stay strong. "Morning is coming, my beloved," I hear Him whisper to my weary soul. Every time I watch the sunrise, the sky painted in cotton candy pinks and purples, I am reminded that the darkness does not last forever. The night may feel overwhelming and painful, but we can trust that God wastes nothing. We can trust He is walking with us through our darkest moments, paving the way for the morning.

> *We can trust He is walking with us through our darkest moments, paving the way for the morning.*

Most painters prepare their canvas by painting one solid color as the base. This can be any color, depending on the subject they are painting and the tonality they hope to portray. Preparing the canvas ensures the paint doesn't get absorbed into the cracks of the canvas while they are painting. Just like the painter prepares his canvas for painting something beautiful, God uses the dark, nighttime moments of our lives to prepare the canvas of our hearts for something beautiful to come. We may not see it now, but we can trust He is working. As long as I've lived, the sun continues to come up each morning. No matter how dark the night feels, I know and trust that light is coming. Just as the sun peeks through my window each morning, the dark days don't last forever. God is working His masterpiece in you and me. If you feel stuck in the darkness, perhaps your canvas isn't ready yet. Trust in the process of God working in your heart and the truth that morning is coming.

When my son was in pre-kindergarten, we went through some major behavioral struggles with him. He would get in trouble most days at school for his busyness and impulsivity, and he would express anger and frustration at home. I was also pregnant with our third baby at the time. I was tired and run down, both emotionally and physically. A typical scene from our home during this season looked like this: my son would get upset about something—it didn't matter what—and anger spewed out of him like bubbling lava. The slightest trigger would send him into a tailspin. One such day, in the middle of a raging meltdown, I picked him up lovingly and carried him to his room, explaining he needed a break and so did Mommy and that I would come back in five minutes to talk to him about his behavior so we could resume our afternoon. I hadn't even gotten the door shut when he started pounding on the door, followed by ear-curdling screams and the crash of things being hurled around his room. As I stumbled down the hall to let him get it out and have his moment, a large, hardcover book came hurtling past my head. I turned around abruptly and yelled at him, telling him he needed to get back in his room until I came in to get him. Because he wouldn't stay in his room and because I was honestly a little fearful of his wrath, both for me and for his baby brother, I ended up removing the door handle from his door until he was calm again. I crawled into my closet and collapsed, weeping ugly tears. With my face buried in my knees, I sobbed and cried out for God to help. I didn't know what to do. I was not prepared for this part of parenting. How do you talk to and handle a little person who is losing their mind?

I wish I could tell you this only happened once, but this season of our parenting lasted longer than I would have hoped. We tried everything under the sun. I read countless books with numerous ideas and theories I hoped would help, but it wasn't until I finally mustered up the courage to ask for help from a professional that we saw actual change in our child. I remember feeling so alone going through this season. If anyone else I knew had ever had a child who had gone through these types of behaviors, they were not open about it. If I ever mentioned it to someone, trying to reach for a lifeline, I typically felt rejected and judged rather than seen or heard.

There was no quick resolution to our son's behavior—it took a lot of time, patience, hard work, and maturity (on all our parts) to get through that season. Five years later, this same child is now ten. He is thriving, and although he still deals with bouts of anger and frustration now and then (as all children do), I can proudly say I have not had a book or any other dangerous object thrown at me in years. We have moved through the season of feeling like we were drowning in his anger, and I can genuinely say that he is one of the coolest kids I know. I can't wait to see how God uses that fire inside of him in the years to come.

The Lord faithfully walked us through that dark season, and now we stand on the other side, stronger, wiser, and more resilient for what lies ahead. God wastes nothing. His faithfulness does not rely on the resolution of our conflicts but rather on our trust in Him. No matter what you face today, whether it be a child with behavioral issues or a scary medical diagnosis that seems to consume your every thought, don't hesitate to ask for help. Remember that God is with you in it. Do not feel ashamed, embarrassed, or like you are failing as a parent because you can't figure this out on your own. On the contrary, asking for help is one of the most courageous things you can do as a parent. Asking for help is not just admitting that you do not know it all—it shows just how deeply you care to set aside your pride and to do whatever is necessary.

Asking for help is one of the most courageous things you can do as a parent.

God doesn't desire for us to sit and wallow in our difficult times. Instead, He invites us into a partnership with Him where He promises true rest in the midst of the difficulties. There are a lot of different definitions of rest out there, but the one I like most that aligns well with the biblical definition comes from Webster's Revised Unabridged Dictionary. It is defined as freedom from everything that worries or disturbs; peace; security. I love this picture of rest because it aligns with the rest Jesus talks about in Matthew 11:28-29.

Are you tired? Worn out? Burned out on religion? Come to me. Get away with me and you'll recover your life. I'll show you how to take a real rest. Walk with me and work with me—watch how I do it. Learn the unforced rhythms of grace.
—MATTHEW 11:28–29, MSG

Jesus talks about spiritual rest, but sometimes spiritual rest comes from physical rest. Do you need a break today, friend? Jesus is inviting you to get away with Him and experience the unforced rhythms of grace and find true rest in His holy presence.

Jesus Himself knows the depths of your heart. He knows what you are facing today, and He invites you to come to Him, walk with Him, and work with Him so He can show you what it means to take a real rest. Real rest offers freedom from whatever it is that is wearying you spiritually. True rest relies on trusting Jesus amid your tired, worn-out life and learning new rhythms. You may have to do things differently than you have been, but in the end, the true rest that Jesus offers brings peace and hope into the darkness. It provides ecurity, knowing that the God of the universe is working, even in the darkest places of your heart, and that He will never let you go. It offers the hope of the sunrise.

Unprepared

Have you ever gone into something feeling unprepared? That question may draw up some faded memories of a pop quiz in high school chemistry that you knew nothing about. One of the biggest things I have ever felt unprepared for was motherhood. I came to the table with no experience or knowledge of what this job entails. I am one of three children in my family, right in the middle, and although my younger sister is nearly five years younger, I didn't come into motherhood with a ton of parenting experience. I don't remember ever helping change her diaper or much about her being a baby. I babysat here and there growing up and even nannied for a family my senior year of college, but that still didn't leave me with much training for the actual job of motherhood. But no matter how much experience you have before becoming a mom, I believe most moms would agree that the majority of days, especially in the beginning, are like flying blind. You don't know what you don't know. Life is the best teacher. This is why I think it is so important for us to share our stories and find others who aren't afraid of sharing the hard and not-so-pretty parts of their journey—so that we can learn from one another.

The boy I nannied in college was a super picky eater. Do you have one of those? All he ate every day for lunch, for almost the whole year I nannied him, was a cheese sandwich. I remember one day attempting to get him to try something new; I snuck some tiny, torn-apart pieces of turkey lunch meat onto his sandwich. It worked for one day, but the next day, he refused to eat it. I remember taking on this challenge for a little bit, trying to make it fun. One day, we ate a whole lunch full of only orange things. Another day, I tried a Lunchable, thinking surely all kids love Lunchables. It wasn't really a healthy option, but I thought we should try something new. It was an uphill battle with this kid, and after a while, I grew weary of the struggle. As a very immature twenty-year-old, I remember saying to myself, *Well it is not my job to get him to eat more than cheese sandwiches. I'm not the mom. If the parents say it is okay, who am I to try to get this kid to eat more variety?* So, I stopped trying.

I still think about this kid now and then. I wish that I hadn't given up trying with him. He is my reminder to never give up on the things that are hard in parenting. Whenever I feel like throwing in the towel, I remember that growth takes time, determination, and perseverance (for my children, but also me). Just as you wouldn't get frustrated with your little toddler learning to walk for the first time, we need to learn to extend this same compassion and grace to ourselves as we are learning to mother for the first time. You will fall down lots of times, but you learn

> *You will fall down lots of times, but you learn to walk by continuing to get back up.*

to walk by continuing to get back up. I am not the same mom or woman I was when I started this journey, and neither are you. We continue to learn and grow, just like our children. If we allow Him, God will use our motherhood journeys, every part of them, as the greatest training ground for our characters and our hearts. All to draw us closer to Him and prepare us for whatever the journey ahead may hold.

Cast Everything

Cast your cares on the LORD and he will sustain you;
he will never let the righteous be shaken.
—PSALM 55:22

In a world that seems to be screaming to pull yourself up by your bootstraps and figure it out on your own, a world that is uncomfortable with all the hard emotions, God pleads for you to bring it all to Him. God wants you to come to Him with your problems, struggles, joys, and sorrow—not just the big things, but the little things as well. He cares about it all and isn't scared of them. God isn't squirming uncomfortably on His throne because you are having a hard day. He wants all of the good days but also all the bad days. He wants it all!

> *God isn't squirming uncomfortably on His throne because you are having a hard day.*

Just recently, I was having quite the morning with my youngest. My husband had been out of town for a few days already, and my sweet daughter had decided that this would be the weekend she would choose to have several manic breakdowns—multiple a day. It was Sunday morning, and as usual, we were getting ready to walk out the door to church. In anticipation of a difficult morning on my own, I tried my best to set myself up to leave early and be on time. Getting dressed and leaving the house has been one of my daughter's major struggles the last couple of years, so I was doing my best to make this a good morning. However, even the best-laid plans. . . Adelle, once again, had a hard time getting ready and out the door, resulting in a frenzy that made for a very distraught child and mommy. By the time we made it to church, I had already reached my capacity for the day. Knowing my children were in good hands, I at least felt I had a moment to breathe and headed toward the sanctuary. After the service, I went to pick up my kiddos from their rooms only to have not one, not two, but three different leaders stop me along the way to tell me how hard my oldest son had been that morning. It was unexpected news, and by the third person, the tears began to flow. I couldn't save face or hold them in any longer. The floodgates opened, and I left feeling more discouraged than when I first got there.

Fast forward to the following weekend. We had a somewhat easier time getting out the door, and all the kids were having a fine morning at Sunday school, so I was shocked and a bit hurt by the individual who stopped me on the way into the church, saying, "It's so nice to see you smiling today." With my heart now in my throat, I nodded and found my seat in the sanctuary. On no other occasion had any of these people seen me cry. I never let them see anything other than my bubbly, cheerful exterior. Yet, in my one moment of having a hard day, of letting down my guard, it was clear that my tears made them uncomfortable, and for weeks after it seemed to be the only thing they remembered about me. I've realized that although we all want the church to be a place where we can come broken, people don't like broken. Brokenness makes them uncomfortable.

I share this story because we all have hard days. We all have moments when we just can't keep up the charade any longer—moments we can't even muster up a fake smile because the day, the month, or the year has just been too hard. Humans will always let you down. Humans will, for whatever reason, always be uneasy with your imperfections. I wish it weren't so, but for now, it is how it seems to be in our world. But, God. God welcomes those imperfect parts of you. He cares about every part of your day and life, and He encourages you to come to Him and cast it all on Him so that He can sustain you, especially in those tough moments. He doesn't expect you to have it all together all the time. In fact, He knows you won't. His only desire is that you come to Him when you are having that hard day. Don't bottle it up. Don't try to muster up the strength on your own. No! Bring it to Him.

"Cast all your cares on the Lord and He will sustain you." The Hebrew word used here for cast is *hashaleke*, meaning *to place*. The root comes from *shalak*, meaning *to abandon or throw off.*[7] God allows you and encourages you to bring whatever is weighing you down to Him —to cast it on Him, to release it, let it go, and abandon it at His feet,

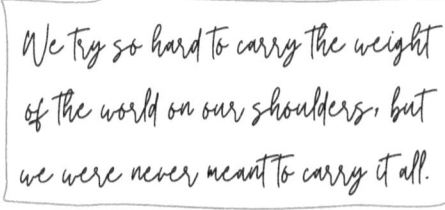

We try so hard to carry the weight of the world on our shoulders, but we were never meant to carry it all.

allowing Him to take the weight of it. We try so hard to carry the weight of the world on our shoulders, but we were never meant to carry it all. Even the weight of all the good things eventually becomes too heavy to bear on our own.

In some versions of the Bible, it is our *burdens* we cast, not our cares. The Hebrew word for *burden, yehavecha,* means *a gift or portion.*[8] We could argue that even our burdens are God's gifts to us. Our cares and burdens are one and the same. My greatest gift is my children, yet some days they do feel like a burden. The weight of raising them feels much too heavy for me to do on my own, and that is because it is. God never asked you or me to do it on our own. The burden feels so heavy because you care so much. That is why it is imperative that we fully learn to entrust whatever it is God has gifted us with to Him. Don't try to carry it all on your own. You were never meant to.

When you release, cast your worries, fears, doubts, failures, all of it on God, He will take the weight from your shoulders. He doesn't bring shame or condemnation but a reprieve from the weight of life you are carrying. He then helps you carry it, sustains you for the road ahead, and offers you rest and peace in Him so that you can carry on.

What is weighing you down today, my friend? Are you dealing with a difficult child? Do you need to make a hard decision? Are you wrestling with feeling physically exhausted and pulled in too many directions? What is it right now that is preoccupying your every thought and disrupting your inner peace? The Lord knows what you are walking through, but an action step still needs to be taken. To cast requires movement on your part. Think of whatever you are carrying as a large stone or a boulder. You may be able to carry it for a while on your own, but over time, that stone becomes heavier and heavier, beginning to weigh you down. To cast your cares or burdens on the Lord is simply to bring them to Him, to take that stone and throw it as far as you can into the sea.

When the hard days and nights seem to drag on forever, with no end in sight, remember to cling to Jesus. When darkness seems to be all you see, cling to the light. Jesus is "the light of the world" (John 8:12), and even the tiniest sliver of light breaks through the darkness. "Whoever follows me will never walk in darkness." (John 8:12) Hang on, my friend. Morning is coming. The darkness will break, and when you release your burdens to the only One capable of carrying their full weight, you will receive rest. A rest that will bring you hope, security, and peace, even when the road ahead is uncertain.

Questions to Ponder

♥ Is there an area in your motherhood journey where you feel alone or in the dark?

♥ Where have you experienced God's faithfulness through a dark season of motherhood?

♥ Where in your motherhood journey have you felt unprepared? What is an area where you have received your training on the job?

Try This

Find a time and space in your daily routine to be alone with God. Watch the sunrise or the sunset. Find a quiet space and recall the times in your life when God has proven to be faithful. Try journaling them or writing them down and re-reading them on a regular basis to remind yourself of what God has carried you through. This is an important exercise. God's track record is one hundred percent.

CHAPTER THREE:

IN THE MESS

Whoever wants to be my disciple must deny themselves and take up their cross daily and follow me. For whoever wants to save their life will lose it, but whoever loses their life for me will save it. What good is it for someone to gain the whole world, and yet lose or forfeit their very self?
Luke 9:23-25

Where the *Wild Things Are* by Maurice Sendak is one of my children's favorite bedtime stories. Even though my children are older now, they still giggle at this story. There is something so relatable to a kid who wants to be wild and free, be in charge, and be the boss–a child who doesn't always want to be good, well-behaved, and told what to do. In the story, a young boy, Max, lets his imagination grow wild when his mom sends him to his room with no supper for causing too much mischief all around the house. He imagines a jungle growing in his room, and he sails away, becoming king of the wild things. But as he lives in his fantasy world, he begins to miss being where someone loves him best of all. He begins to long for home. So, he waves goodbye to the wild things and journeys back to his room, where his supper awaits him.

I can relate so much to Max in this story. There have been many times in my life where I feel like God puts parameters on me that I don't love, and I imagine a world where things would be different. I grumble at my circumstances and wish I could sail away from all of life's troubles. I find myself seeking escapes from real life, whether in a book, a vacation, or by numbing out in front of a screen. It seems innocent enough, but when the false realities start to look more appealing than your real ones, you begin tiptoeing into dangerous territory.

When life feels out of control, I like to hold on to the reins even tighter. I have to be reminded over and over to let go and trust God. He tenderly reminds me that what I already have is good, and my heart longs for a place where I am loved and feel safe. My heart longs for home—home with Jesus.

We each have eternity written on our hearts—a longing for a future home, an eternal home with Him in heaven. A home where we feel loved most of all. A home filled with good food to eat, where we get to spend eternity living in the presence of our Creator. Where there is no more pain or suffering, no more tears, and all will praise and worship our Lord and King forever (Rev. 21:4). There is nothing more beautiful. Nothing is more fulfilling. Nothing is more satisfying.

I believe this is the reason we as humans search high and low for beautiful places here on Earth. We search for meaning and a sense of belonging to something bigger than ourselves. Contrary to what the world may say, you don't need to search across the globe to find this fulfillment. God has imprinted "home" in your soul and on your heart. He is the only One who will truly satisfy the longing, and one day, He will take us to our perfect home. What a glorious day it will be for all believers when we are reunited with our Savior and Creator.

Do you live your life searching for something more? Do you find yourself living vicariously through others on social media? Were you hoping motherhood would fill some void in your heart, but now you feel like you're drowning? Motherhood was never meant to satisfy what only God can. Nothing we can achieve, buy, acquire, or make should ever take God's place in our hearts.

Motherhood was never meant to satisfy what only God can.

Living in this world, especially in the West, and keeping an eternal perspective is difficult. It is so easy to grumble about our circumstances that feel overwhelming at the moment, forgetting about the long game. I toil about the house all day, cleaning and cooking, and then find myself irritated by the fifteen seconds it takes my kids to ravage a room. Too often, I find myself mindlessly numbing out on social media, escaping to some grand adventure or in someone else's glamorous life. Please tell me I'm not alone here. Our souls were not meant for this continuous wandering. Our hearts were designed intricately and intimately to be at home with our Creator. We will never find true rest toiling about or numbing out.

Just as guardrails are put on the side of the road so that cars do not tumble over the side of a mountain, we, too, must put guardrails up in our lives so that we are protected from going over the edge and crashing into dissatisfaction and discontentment. God desires to give you rest from the persistent wandering, and it starts with wanting more of Him and making sure He is first and foremost above it all. It is okay in and of itself to have nice things, want to take nice vacations, or have a clean home. It is when you start to put these things above what is truly important, that you may feel discontent with your life. You know you have stepped over the edge when these things become an idol in your heart. These good things in your life were never meant to fill the part of your heart and soul that is only meant for God. If you feel discontented, empty, easily triggered, or like you are in a perpetual state of striving, it may be time to check your heart and honestly assess where these things stand in your life.

An idol is a very religious word and can feel obscure. But to put it simply, an idol is anything we hold above God. Sometimes, this happens unintentionally, especially for us as moms. Sometimes, our idols are the good things in our lives, like our children, spouses, or jobs. It can be very easy to put our children or ourselves above time with God, but to experience a true heart at rest, we must put no other things above God—not even good things.

Has motherhood become an idol in your heart? Have your children taken priority over your time with God? Has your home taken priority over time with God? Maybe your body? Archbishop William Temple said it best: "Your religion is what you do with your solitude."[9] What is it that you and I do with our solitude? Where have I unintentionally raised idols in my life? This pricks my heart in such a good way. It is a worthy challenge posed to check my heart.

I have often unintentionally prioritized my kids' schedules and activities above my time with God. I've picked up my phone and scrolled through social media first thing in the morning before opening my Bible or spending time in prayer. Just this morning, as I sat down in my typical chair to do my quiet time, I saw an email from a scholarship program I had been working on for months, informing me my application needed more documents and was now closed. It derailed my time with God and consumed my entire morning as I waited on hold with the organization, gathered documents, and went to Office Depot to fax them. It threw me into a funky head space all morning, and to be honest, I was irritated, frustrated, and overwhelmed all day long. As I sit down to write, it is not lost on me that here I am, re-reading and continuing to write about idols and priorities. These words are just as much for me as they are for you because we all need them—every day.

Mama, I know you are trying hard to give your kids a wonderful home that is safe, loving, clean, healthy, and a place they know they can always come back to. I know you are trying to manage friendships, date nights, and sports schedules. Remember to put God first when life feels overwhelming, when you feel discouraged, or when you are constantly striving for more and more. Remove the distractions that are calling for your attention, even if it is just for ten minutes. Take a breath. God is faithful and promises to give you the true rest you are craving, the rest that encompasses your heart and soul as you remember to put Him back on the throne of your heart.

Bless the Mess

Just like Max became king of the wild things, when you and I became moms, we were promoted to queens of all the wild things. We learn new languages, how to tame these tiny beasts (which doesn't always work by just staring at them without blinking, although I'll admit, it does work sometimes), and how to do new dances and find new rhythms of life with our little wild things running around all the time. It isn't picture-perfect. There is no one-size-fits-all. The rhythms of your family are assuredly different from mine, and the messes that transpire in my home probably aren't the messes

> *Life will throw you curveball after curveball, with the occasional strikeout, but also the rare home run.*

that occur in yours. But rest assured, it is messy. Life will throw you curveball after curveball, with the occasional strikeout, but also the rare home run.

When I had my first son and went back to school after a brief maternity leave, I remember coming home from a full day to the house in complete disarray. There were toys strewn across the floor in every room, dishes in the sink, piles of laundry waiting to be done, and dinner waiting to be cooked. I scrambled around the house, picking up toys and throwing them in bins before jumping straight into feeding the baby, followed by trying to make a meal for my husband and me. It was utter madness for about an hour and a half when I got home. This was the routine almost every day. It left me physically and mentally drained, and I only had one kid at the time. Fast-forward to three kids, and at times, it still feels this wild. More kids mean more messes and lots more meals. It continues to feel unattainable to contain the chaos of my home, yet I faithfully strive to do so.

It has taken me a long time to embrace the messiness of motherhood. I'm still a work in progress, but just as I have needed to flip the script when comparing myself to other moms, I have learned to flip the script regarding the messes and shift my focus from the hard to the blessing. The reality is that life with kids is messy. It takes intentionality, but I try to remind myself daily of the blessings and the value in the messes. When the playroom is an utter disaster, instead of walking by and wanting to throw every toy away or donate them to charity, I'm reminded that the kids are busy making memories and using their imaginations. Sometimes, we all get together and clean the mess. Other times, I intentionally choose to close the door and walk away. They are building and learning, which is much more important than a clean playroom. Although I must admit (and my husband can attest), I still throw a *lot* of things away from time to time.

When you view the messes of motherhood through the lens of the blessings from which they come, you can learn to soak up the joy in this very brief season of life. All too soon, the days will come when your home will be cleaner and quieter, and you will look around and long for the return of these days. As hard and exhausting as these days are, you must learn to live in them instead of being broken by them.

The pitter-patter of little feet running down the hall or the belly laughs from a silly game you've invented in the bathtub, or the pain from stepping on a Lego guy's head stuck in the carpet - there will come a day when these things will no longer be common in our homes. I don't want either of us to miss the value in them now. Don't miss the beauty of the moment you are living in because you are too distracted by the messes. Let the dishes sit in the sink for a moment longer and play that game of Candyland or shoot hoops in the driveway. To find joy in this season, embrace the mess and take time to play. You don't have to live in utter chaos to embrace the messiness of this season. You absolutely can and should create structure and set boundaries in your home. But allow the kids to help with the cleanup and empower them to be a part of the process. More kids mean more messes, but more kids also mean more helping hands. Let go of what you can let go of and cling to the truth that Jesus is fully present with you, even in the mess.

> *Don't miss the beauty of the moment you are living in because you are too distracted by the messes.*

Have you ever had a last-minute guest call telling you they are coming over for a visit? If you are like me and want the house to look somewhat presentable before they arrive, you find yourself in a panic, scrambling from room to room, throwing clutter into bins or bags and then hiding them in the closet. Your guest arrives and is in awe at how tidy you keep your house on a regular basis. *Ha! Just don't open that door there*, you think to yourself. How often do we feel the need to clean ourselves up before we let Jesus in? How often do I feel the need to do the dishes before I can sit down and open my Bible for some quiet time?

Jesus wants to be a part of your every day. He isn't waiting for your home to be picture-perfect or your life to be put all together to be with you. He is with you in whatever season you are in, no matter what state your house is in. Don't put your time with Jesus off until later because of the seemingly important messes that need to be cleaned up. Instead, invite Him inside, even when the house is a mess or your life feels like a mess.

Jesus tenderly asks for you to "walk with [Him] and work with [Him]—watch how [He] does it" (Matt. 11:29, MSG). This means bringing

Him into the mess and allowing Him into all your life's unpleasant, painful, and messy places while watching and learning His ways. As you do, He has promised to teach you how to live freely and lightly and what it means to take a real rest—not rest from the housework or your other daily duties, but a true rest for your soul that will allow you to feel peace even in the messiness of motherhood.

Where there are no oxen, the manger is empty.
—PROVERBS 14:4

As a bit of a type-A perfectionist personality, clutter and messes make my skin crawl. I can't help it. I'm not sure if this was an inherited quality (thanks, Mom), but this came to be a part of me, and it has been a huge stressor for me as a mom. This verse speaks so sweetly to my heart, and I believe it speaks to many mamas struggling to keep our homes neat and tidy while our children still live in them. Through this verse, I hear God whispering to my heart, "Hey, mama, don't forget people still live in your home." Maybe you are like me and find yourself growing weary of cleaning the same messes day after day and constantly doing dishes and laundry. Let this be a sweet reminder that as long as people are living in your home, there will be proof that you all live there. So, unless you are going to send the kids, your husband and the dogs packing, there may be some messes in your home.

How many times a day are we bombarded with images of idyllic homes, stunningly beautiful living spaces, and extremely organized playrooms or pantries? While these images are pretty and appealing to my organization-loving heart, they can start to wear me down after a while if I'm not careful. Scrolling through Pinterest has often left me feeling discontent rather than inspired, especially as I simultaneously stare at the pile of laundry still sitting at the end of my bed, waiting to be folded.

Clearly, I am not alone in this matter, as more and more research shows that the more time we spend on social media, the more our life satisfaction levels decline over time.[10] We have to be very careful not only of how much time we spend on these social media apps but also of who we follow and how we internalize the information. Reflect on the last couple of weeks. How much time have you spent on social media? Do you generally feel more satisfied with your life after spending time on social media, or do you tend to feel dissatisfied or discontent? It is important we don't base our self-worth on what we see on social media.

Suppose you were to walk into my home right now. In that case, this is what you would find on most days: a relatively clean house, a candle burning on my living room coffee table, dishes drying on the rack by the sink, and most likely a pile of kids' belongings sitting on the dining room table waiting to be put away, and overflowing shoe baskets by the front door. There is probably some sort of science project left on the back patio and definitely laundry going in the laundry room. If you walk into my home right now, there would be no doubt that people actually live here. It doesn't look like a curated space on social media; it is real, and the proof of humans dwelling in this space is part of its charm.

Mama, it is okay that your home doesn't look like the cover of a magazine. What you see on Instagram and Pinterest is carefully assembled and staged. It is not real life. Your real life is beautiful because of the people who live within your walls, not because of what is hanging on them. There is nothing wrong with wanting to have a beautiful, clean home. It is when the home becomes more important than those living in it, when the cleaning of the mess trumps the ones who are making the mess, that discontentment and dissatisfaction creep in to steal your joy and rob you of true rest.

> Your real life is beautiful because of the people who live within your walls, not because of what is hanging on them.

Practically speaking, there are a few things that I try to do to stay present and not let the messes steal my joy. First and foremost, I try to read my Bible and get into God's Word daily. Most days, I do this first thing in the morning, but other days, it happens at midday or right before bed. I find it rewarding to wake up, start my quiet time, and have a little one wake up and join me on the couch. Instead of letting this get me discouraged or flustered, I try to invite them into my time with God. We snuggle up close, and they see a mama who prioritizes spending time with Jesus. I once heard that the best way to disciple our children is by showing them. So, let your kids see you reading God's Word. Show them what it looks like to follow Jesus and need Jesus every day. This will not only impact your faith and ability to let go of perfectionism, but it will surely impact your kids as well.

Another big thing that has helped me overcome the feelings of dissatisfaction in my own home is to stay off social media—or at least limit my time on it. Although social media is a fantastic tool when used appropriately to reach others around the globe, I've noticed in my own life that the more time I spend on it, the more easily frustrated I seem to become. The more time I spend on a device, the more distracted I am from what is right in front of me, and the more likely I am to want or desire something I don't have. It's a double-edged sword. One way I manage my time spent on social media is by using app timers. I try to limit my time to thirty or forty minutes a day, which still feels like a lot. I also have my phone set to go into sleep mode between 10:30 p.m. and 5:30 a.m. It turns the screen black and white and reminds me to put down the phone if I find myself mindlessly scrolling too late into the evening.

I know this sounds simple and self-explanatory, and I may not be sharing anything you don't already know. However, if you struggle with social media use and feeling discontent, I truly believe the best thing you can do is get off it. Try taking a complete social media break every once in a while. I've done this a few times; it is so freeing and healing. Guess what? The world keeps spinning. And it makes me actually reach out to my friends instead of just liking their posts or seeing their stories. Whether for a weekend, a week, a month, or longer, it feels good to turn the noise level down and get back to being present in your life.

One last thing that has really helped me over the years is implementing a "time blocking" schedule when it comes to housework. I used to clean all the time, no matter what. But in recent years, with bigger kids and more chaotic schedules, I've had to find a new rhythm of cleaning that doesn't take up every second of my free time. Time blocking is the idea of allocating chunks of time to related tasks. For example, on days that I am not going to work after dropping the kids off at school, I designate the first forty-five minutes after drop off to clean up all the chaos of the morning. I do the dishes from breakfast, do a quick clean of any surfaces in the main areas of the house, and, most days, do a quick vacuum of the floors during this block. Two days a week, I allot another sixty minutes to do laundry and clean the bathrooms. And once a week, typically on Saturday, the whole family works on cleaning and tidying up all the bedrooms, along with any outside work.

During this time, I typically practice something called habit stacking. I will listen to a podcast or audiobook while I do my housework. It helps me work more efficiently and allows me to be filled up while I am working. Sometimes, I blare worship music. It is my way to invite Jesus into my mess and my mundane day. It helps keep my mind focused on what is important and disrupts the thoughts of dissatisfaction and discontentment that so easily creep in.

This isn't a perfect system; I could probably designate a whole chapter to this topic. However, the point is to find a system that works for you. Find blocks of time or chunks throughout your day when you can be consistent with the cleaning, and then let it go the rest of the day. The messes will continue to happen, so you don't want to let them go forever, but the realization that kids make messes and create clutter is something you have to accept and overcome. I may still be working on this realization myself.

Jesus wants to be invited into your mess. He sees the dust bunnies gathering under the beds and the pee on the side of the toilet you just cleaned yesterday. He isn't judging or criticizing you. He isn't avoiding your home because it doesn't look like the cover of *Better Homes & Gardens*. Jesus doesn't want you to wait until your home is perfect or your life *looks* put together to come to Him. He wants you to invite Him in now. Invite Him into the mess. Praise and worship Him, even in the mess.

> When you invite Jesus into your chaos, He can hold it all together, so you don't have to.

True rest can be found when you understand the blessings within the messes—when you give yourself grace for the hard days and lean into Jesus' presence even amongst the disorder. When you feel like you can't keep up with everything, He sees your heart and your effort. Do your best and remind yourself the messes that drive you so crazy are the result of those things you love so dearly. Your home could maybe be a little tidier and quieter only if the children were not there. So, embrace the mess. Live fully present, knowing you don't have to have it all together. When you invite Jesus into your chaos, He can hold it all together, so you don't have to. As you let go, He is faithful in bringing your heart rest from the weariness, the true rest and peace that only He can give.

Perfectionist Meet "Real Mom"

But Martha was distracted by all the preparations that had to be made. She came to him and asked, "Lord, don't you care that my sister has left me to do the work by myself? Tell her to help me!"

"Martha, Martha," the Lord answered, "you are worried and upset about many things, but few things are needed—or indeed only one. Mary has chosen what is better, and it will not be taken from her.
—LUKE 10:40–42

Have you ever felt like Martha, tending to and worrying about many things in preparation for a party or event? Maybe you are worried and upset about many things within your regular day. It is so easy to get caught up in all of the to-dos of the day that we completely forget what is indeed the only thing that is needed—to sit at the feet of Jesus, listen to His words, and soak up His presence. I love Jesus' tenderness in His response to Martha. He acknowledges her worry and hard work but then gently reminds her that she doesn't need to do everything that she is doing. He sweetly tells her that He will not tell Mary to get up and help her, as she has chosen, out of the many things she could be doing, "what is better" (Luke 10:42).

I am just like Martha—a full-blown, people-pleasing busybody, a can't-sit-still perfectionist. I love hosting parties and gatherings. I love inviting people into my home and creating a space for others to feel warm and welcome. Hospitality is something that means a lot to our family. But sometimes, I can get caught up in everything that needs to be done and neglect what is truly important. In my desire for everything to be just right, wishing to please and serve those around me, I miss out on enjoying the people around me.

Can you relate? You may be a Mary, and you can set aside the task list to enjoy your guests or, in many cases, your children. But if you are more like me, more of a Martha by nature, you tend to be more concerned about all the things that need to get done and end up missing the moment right in front of you. Jesus saw Martha in this situation, and He sees you, too. He appreciates everything you are doing, but through this story, we are reminded not to forget what is truly important: spending quality time with Him and the people around us.

There is no such thing as a perfect mom. There is no one right way to do this whole mothering thing. Each child brings something new and different to the table, so we must keep growing and adapting as the seasons change. The best mom is a healthy mom who has her priorities in the right place and can take the things that are worrying and upsetting her and bring them to the feet of Jesus. When you do this, He can fill up your cup so you can pour it out on the ones you love. I think this is what Jesus was trying to remind Martha of in this story—and through it, us as well. He wants us to make sure our hearts are in the right place and to put Him first. Jesus loves when we serve others, and we are commanded to do so as believers, but we must make sure we are serving from the right place in our hearts—from a place of love and reverence for Him.

Do you feel lost in all the to-dos of your day? Is your task list spilling over and stealing your joy in motherhood? Mama, I have been there, and want you to know you are not alone. Yes, there will be days when you must clean the house around your kids or fold laundry while your toddler throws Cheerios to the dog from the highchair. It will feel exhausting and overwhelming, but don't let those feelings that come from looking over the to-do list rob you of this beautiful season. If you feel worried and upset about many things, remember what is truly important. Remember Jesus' tender words here, that there is "indeed only one" thing that is needed, and that is Him (Luke 10:42).

True rest is found when you sit at the feet of Jesus as Mary did, soaking up everything He has to say as He offers to lighten your burdens. As you learn His ways, He helps you be the best mom, friend, spouse, daughter that you can be. He releases you from the clutches of perfectionism and the need for everything to be "just so" when you come to Him and spend time with Him. Jesus is the only One capable of filling the empty holes in your heart and offering you rest from the busyness of life. When you find time to spend in His Word, to be with Him in all the moments of your day, even the messy ones, His presence will offer you true rest—rest your soul is so desperately craving.

Questions to Ponder

- ♥ Is there an area in your mothering where you are seeking earthly recognition or praise?

- ♥ How are you living today in light of eternity?

- ♥ Is there a time during the day when you feel overwhelmed by the messes in your house? What is one thing you can do to feel less stressed about the mess?

- ♥ Read Luke 10:38-42. As you read the story of Mary and Martha, who do you resonate with more? Why?

Try This

Once a day, try to pause the chores while the kids are home and play with them. Find something fun to do together, whether a board game or a game of tag in the backyard. Color with some sidewalk chalk in the driveway or go on a walk together. Find some way to stop worrying about all the to-dos and enjoy this beautiful time you have with your little (or big) ones.

CHAPTER FOUR:
BEAUTY IN THE MUNDANE

Whatever you do, work at it with all your heart, as working for the
Lord, not for human masters.
Colossians 3:23

An Audience of One

It had been a long day at work—twelve hours laboring on my feet at the salon. I came home exhausted, just wanting to put my feet up, flop my body onto the couch, and numb out after an exhausting day behind the chair. When I walked through the door, I looked around to find dirty dinner dishes still in the sink, toys scattered on the floor in the entryway, and the pillows on the couch disheveled—probably from a toddler pillow fight. My heart sank.

I made my way to the sink, where I started washing the dishes and putting them in the dishwasher. I felt my body tense when I heard my husband coming down the hall from tucking the kids in bed. I tried to hide my frustration and greeted him with a smile and kiss, but inside, I was steaming. After serving clients all day, I didn't have much left to give to my family. I knew in my head that my husband had done a lot himself. He had also worked all day, then picked the kids up, fed them, and got them ready for bed. Yet, for some reason, I thought of how nice it would have been to come home and be done for the day.

The next morning, I found myself fiercely throwing laundry from the washer to the dryer. I thought to myself, *Why do I have to do everything?* I knew this was a lie the moment the thought flew across my mind, but it is how I felt in the moment. The lie spun around in my head, making me feel even more exasperated all morning. I felt overworked and underappreciated, but instead of asking for help, I just stewed in my frustration and took it out on the wet pair of pants I was flinging into the dryer. I am not proud of the woman I was in this season of life. She was angry and bitter all the time. But God, in His goodness, never leaves us in our disheveled state. He calls us out of our sin to change. He spoke some hard truths into my soul in this season, and it was just what I needed to hear. He spoke sweetly and clearly to my heart, reminding me, *Morgan, do it for Me.*

The phrase "Audience of One" was originally coined and used for Christian athletes to remember in all areas of life, even in a stadium full of people, to live, play, and perform in pursuit of God's pleasure above all else. I love how American football player Carson Wentz puts it: "What does Audience of One mean to us? It means that we are playing for an Audience of One. When the lights go on and all eyes are fixed on us, our eyes are fixed on Him: Jesus, the Creator of the universe. It's not just a slogan, it's a lifestyle. Living for Him, playing for Him, and giving Him all the glory. Win, lose, or draw—I play for an Audience of One."[11]

> "When the lights go on and all eyes are fixed on us, our eyes are fixed on Him: Jesus, the Creator of the universe. It's not just a slogan, it's a lifestyle?"

I had to make this mind shift and attitude change in my mothering and in the ordinary tasks that make up so much of my days. As moms, just like athletes on the field, we have many eyes on us—not just the little ones that live beside us, but the others that look at us from the sidelines. In our social-media-crazed culture, we must stand firm on the truth that our worth and value do not come from anything other than our Creator. When you feel invisible, know you are seen by the One who knows the number of hairs on your head. When you feel rejected or alone, know you are loved by the One who formed you in your mother's womb. Your audience is the One who truly matters, and He sees you, adores you, and is cheering you on.

This heart change did not happen overnight for me. It was a slow process and still takes daily intentionality. When I wake up in the morning, I remind myself to posture my heart this way. Jesus teaches in John 15:13 that "there is no greater love than to lay down one's life for one's friends." Laying down your life doesn't have to mean literally dying (although I know all of us mama bears would lay down our lives in a second for our kiddos). Rather, it means laying aside your selfish desires for the sake of someone else—in this case, your kids. What is it that holds you in selfishness? Maybe it's pride. Do you always want things done your way or the highway? Maybe it's your time. Do you selfishly feel this is your time and you should be able to spend it how you want? Most days, for me, it looks like laying down my own expectations as to how I hope a situation will go and choosing to serve my family with humility and joy, no matter what, for an Audience of One.

Motherhood is a selfless and thankless job, but not all your hard work goes unnoticed. I want to encourage you and remind you that your Heavenly Father sees you, and He recognizes everything that you do, day in and day out. Even the things that no one else notices don't go unseen by Him. He not only sees you but is there with you. It brings a smile to His face to watch you labor out of love instead of bitterness. The One who clothes the hillside with beautiful wildflowers and cares for the birds of the air also cares for you. You may not feel it sometimes, but I promise God is always with you.

Remember that living for an Audience of One is a lifestyle. It means doing all the mundane tasks while being aware of God's holy presence in the midst of it. It means focusing your attention on Him instead of performing for others. It means not trying to earn His favor or applause but simply resting in the knowledge that He is your perfect Father, cheering you on from the sidelines. It doesn't mean that you will never fail or feel anxious. It does mean that no matter what the day brings you— whether it's blow-out diapers, raging hormones, or a scary diagnosis from the doctor—you have power and access to God's holy presence amid the trials and turbulence of the day.

Paul writes, "Do everything without grumbling or arguing" (Phil. 2:14). God encourages and challenges my mama heart to do the mundane tasks of life for Him, not for anyone else—for an Audience of One. He encourages me not to let bitterness or discontent build up in my heart when all of my hard work seems to go unnoticed by those around me, or when only twenty minutes after deep cleaning the house you can't tell you even cleaned it—because let's be honest, the children still live here. The truth of the matter is that God sees me and you. He sees the effort. And most importantly, He sees your heart. I challenge you today to really look at where your heart is. Are you serving your family with joy and gratitude or from a place of resentment and bitterness?

> *Are you serving your family with joy and gratitude or from a place of resentment and bitterness?*

Remind yourself who the true audience is and work with all your heart for Him. There is rest to be found when you stop toiling for others and truly live your life with an Audience of One mentality.

With the seeming addiction to social media, it can feel like your life is always on stage. And although it is, in a way, because someone is always watching (i.e., your kids), who do you feel is most important? Do you find yourself curating moments to post on social media? Do you crave more likes and follows from complete strangers over the much simpler praise of your family, and even more importantly, your Heavenly Father? Your family and life don't need to be played out on a big stage to feel significant. God already sees it all.

The world will turn on you in an instant, especially when you say something they don't like or do something the culture deems "wrong." It is impossible to always make everyone happy, so choose who matters most. When you aren't trying to win the applause and favor of the world, you can shift your focus to the One who will love you despite your flaws and failures. The world (other humans) will always let you down, but God never will. You can find true rest as you seek to please the Father instead of the world around you.

Lost in Laundry

Just as we seek to have an Audience of One with the big things in our lives, we should also attempt to have this mentality with the smaller, monotonous daily tasks, like laundry or dishes. When you have three kids, a husband, and a dog, the laundry is never-ending. After I finally get all the baskets washed, folded, and sometimes even put away, I turn around, and somehow the baskets are full again. Is this a cruel joke my family is playing on me? Where does it all come from? Seriously, I still can't quite figure this one out.

It can feel wearisome in the little years of motherhood. You're picking up the same messes twenty times a day, sweeping the floor under the highchair after every meal and snack time, changing diapers endlessly, and piling the other household chores that never end on top. You wake up, do all the things, put the kids to bed, go to sleep, wake up, and do it all over again, day after day. It is an endless cycle of household duties, changing diapers, and making sure your little humans are safe, loved, happy, and still alive at the end of the day.

A part of me slowly died while surviving the monotony of the little years. My days felt like they were in a repetitive loop with no end in sight. What was the purpose? But God, in His goodness, like He always does, spoke to my heart in this season. As the years went by, my children grew, I matured, and God continued to remind me that motherhood is a calling. As John Ortberg says in *If You Want to Walk on Water, You've Got to Get Out of the Boat,* "A calling requires pain."[12] Yes, sometimes motherhood can feel painful and insignificant, but the humdrum of even a regular day in your life as a mom is a true kingdom calling. The laundry may feel endless and overwhelming, but perhaps this is where God is meeting you today. Perhaps this is where you and God get to have your time together—in the simplicity of the little things.

> *Sometimes motherhood can feel painful and insignificant, but the humdrum of even a regular day in your life as a mom is a true kingdom calling.*

The maker of the stars is a God of order. He delights in the extravagant, but oh, how He delights in the small things as well. Just as the atom is fundamental for life, your mundane moments are essential to running your home and raising your family. You don't have to be on a mountaintop to hear God's voice or be the CEO of a Fortune 500 company to be important. God meets you and is with you in the ordinary. He celebrates the ordinary, repetitive days. You should, too!

So many times, I have missed God's tenderness and loving whispers because I have been too caught up in the busyness of my routines and schedules. I have missed His reminders to slow down and soak it all in before it's gone because there were dishes to do or bathrooms to clean. Many times, God is speaking to our hearts through sweet, random moments of our ordinary days—in an "I love you, Mommy" from your toddler, when the baby falls asleep in your arms, or when the sick child wants you to snuggle and tickle his back. I wish I hadn't missed so much of my children's little years worrying about all the other things that needed to be done, but I still have a chance, and so do you. If you have kids still at home, let me encourage you to soak it all up. It's never too late to start embracing the season you are in and appreciate it.

Don't get lost in the laundry or the dishes today, my friend. Instead, let those things be a beautiful opportunity for you to recognize the blessings in your life. Do everything as if unto the Lord. Do not let the mundane, simple moments pass you by. Be right here, present in the life God has given you. As we watch how Jesus lived out His days and ministry, we see He didn't skimp on the little things. He didn't pass over ordinary people living ordinary, average lives. He used those people to change the world! You, mama, are changing the world one diaper change and one load of laundry at a time. True rest doesn't come from removing these things from your plate but from shifting the focus from the task itself to the people and the One you are doing the tasks for. When you make this mind shift, God fills your heart with the peace and understanding that even the little things do not go unnoticed. He sees you and is with you, cheering you on every step of the way.

> *Be right here, present in the life God has given you.*

From the Garden

> *Let us not become weary in doing good, for at its proper time*
> *we will reap a harvest if we do not give up.*
> *—GALATIANS 6:9*

A couple of years ago, I decided to try my hand at gardening. I spent hours researching which plants would grow best in our hot Florida climate and which plants I should ideally plant adjacent to others or separated to ensure the best harvest. Just like parenting, gardening takes time, patience, and a lot of work, and you never quite feel like you've got it figured out—at least, that has been my experience. You plant seeds or sprouts in the early spring to reap a harvest in the summer or fall. You follow all the right steps, but still, sometimes, a critter comes along and steals your harvest in the middle of the night. I have labored long and hard in my garden, and sometimes I have felt like giving up, but I am not a quitter, so I refuse to let the climate, soil, or pests get the better of me. I have had some good harvests and some failures. I have had to pull out entire crops that have gone bad for one reason or another, and then I have reaped full, bountiful harvests when I continue on and don't give up.

The same can be said for us as moms. It can feel overwhelming and exhausting going about your normal life and doing the everyday tasks of motherhood. You can spend hours reading all the books and doing all the things and still not end up with the results you were hoping for. It can leave you weary, worn out, and maybe a little bitter. But mama, you are called to continue doing the good work. When you feel weary, bring it to Jesus. Let Him be the One who shows you the next steps. Don't allow the weariness to defeat you; let it be an opportunity to seek God more fully and an avenue to draw you closer to Him. You will see the fruit of your hard work not only in your children but also in yourself. God is working on you in the midst of it all. Some crops take longer to reap a harvest, but that doesn't mean the work is in vain.

Another important lesson I've learned in my short duration of gardening is the importance of letting the soil "rest." This means pulling everything out of the garden and letting it remain unplanted for a while. This helps restore the soil's natural nutrient balance, breaks the breeding cycles of insect pests, and allows time to amend the soil. If you continue to plant over and over again without resting the soil, there will be no nutrients left in the soil to nourish your crops. It is truly imperative to the success of the plants.

Mama, you need a break sometimes. It is okay to rest your soil if you know what I mean. It is okay to leave the dishes in the sink. It is okay to say "no" to the birthday party. You don't need my permission, but if it helps, let me say you have permission to take a break every once in a while. Without resting your soul, you will eventually be out of nutrients and be good for no one. Just as resting the soil is vital to sustaining the plants in my garden, resting your soul is essential to the health of your mind, body, and spirit.

I have seen so much growth in myself over the years in areas of my life that felt icky, like anger, selfishness, and pride. There wasn't an "aha" moment per se, but more of a gradual growth over time. I read a quote that has stuck with me for years: "The only time you should ever look back is to see how far you've come."[13] I see my growth as I look back and notice how the woman I am today is different. I am not perfect by any means, and there is work to be done in these areas (and others) until the day Jesus calls me home. Just like the garden takes daily work to keep it thriving, so does my heart, and so does yours.

> "The only time you should ever look back is to see how far you've come."

If you are in a season of drought or feel like there's no harvest in sight, keep pressing on, continuing to do the good work given to you, knowing that in its proper time—God's perfect time—He will see it through. Perhaps He is leading you into a season of rest. He is the perfect gardener and knows what is needed to reap a bountiful harvest. You can trust Him. Whether you are in a season of planting, laboring, resting, or harvesting, God is with you through it all. Allow Him the opportunity to provide you with exactly what you need in His way and His time.

Jesus in the Ordinary

My kids and I play a fun little game each day as they go to school, and I go to work: we go on a Jesus hunt. What is a Jesus hunt, you ask? It is simply to be on the lookout for Jesus as you go about your day. It can be how you see someone else being Jesus towards you or how you can be Jesus to someone else. It is so sweet and encourages my kids to find Jesus in the ordinary. It also encourages me and helps me intentionally seek out those moments. It can be as simple as a friend saying something kind to my kids or helping them figure out a math problem. Perhaps they help someone pick up a pile of papers they dropped. It is a sweet reminder for them and me to go about the day searching for Jesus in the simplest ways.

Hearing the reports when we come together around the dinner table later in the evening is always fun. I hope that instilling this practice for them now will encourage them to continue seeing the world this way as they get older.

On one specific occasion, I remember our family sitting down together for dinner, and I asked the kids, "So, did anyone see Jesus today? Or was anyone able to be Jesus today?" My sweet, little four-year-old daughter was quick to be the first to share. She is full of gumption and joy, and the emotions captured in this little human captivate me regularly. She blurted out that she was Jesus to her friend at school because she played tag at recess when she didn't want to. It was so simple and so sweet, yet utterly profound. How could this small child get the simple fact that being Jesus in this world doesn't have to be grand and extravagant? Jesus is clearly found in the grand and extravagant gestures, but He is more profoundly in the quiet, ordinary ones. In the simple kindness of giving up what you want to do to make someone else happy. You never know the impact one act of kindness could have on someone.

Jesus is clearly found in the grand and extravagant gestures, but He is more profoundly in the quiet, ordinary ones.

We've had many such conversations and answers to these questions over the years. The most popular way my kiddos find Jesus in their days is through someone else's kindness. I look forward to hearing their answers evolve as they grow, but my heart tells me that this truly is the best way to approach the hunt—through kindness and humility. What is something nice you have done for someone recently? Has there been someone close to you or perhaps a stranger who has shown you extra kindness today?

The world can feel dark and dreary most days, but practicing finding Jesus throughout your day can change your perspective and outlook on the world around you. When I look for Jesus throughout my day, He really isn't that hard to find. He is always there, sometimes just waiting in the background for you to notice Him. I've had many instances that some may call coincidence, but I see them as divine. One example was when our dog passed away a couple of years ago. If you are a dog person, you know how utterly terrible it is to say goodbye to a fur baby. Kono was my husband's dog in college and had lived a good, long life. He was there when my husband and I got married and there for the birth of every child. He was there through many of life's ups and downs, and it broke our hearts to say goodbye to him. My very best friend decided to bring our family dinner and leave it on our counter while we all were out at school and work. It was nothing crazy, but this sweet, heartfelt act is one way I have experienced Jesus in the ordinary. I could have just thanked her and moved on but knowing that this was a way Jesus used someone in my life to comfort me, I have been able to pay this forward to others around me. Jesus isn't just there with us in our pain—He works in it, sometimes through the kind actions of others around us.

My kids and I don't always get this right. They are still learning to keep their hands to themselves and use kind words with each other and with friends. I am still learning not to explode when something goes awry in the house or to not get snippy with my husband when I am overwhelmed. But the more we each search for Jesus in our ordinary and look for opportunities to be Jesus throughout our days, the more natural it becomes to be the hands and feet of Christ, to live out our faith, and to be a light to those around us. God delights as we learn and choose to be more like Him. In our ordinary, simple lives, He calls us to live for Him, knowing that our simple, everyday encounters with others and with our children can make a great impact. The ripple effect goes far beyond what you can see.

When Jesus promises to show us how to take a real rest, He asks us to first come to Him and then to walk with Him and work with Him (Matt. 11:28–30). To come to Him, we must seek Him. To walk and work with Him, we must study His ways and invite Him into our ordinary lives. It takes intentionality and effort. There are a lot of things grasping for your attention, dear mama. Do your everyday tasks as if you were working for the Lord, and not only will you find more satisfaction in the tasks, but you will also find Jesus in everything you do. Your heart will find real rest, even in the regular, ordinary moments of your day.

Take Delight

Trust in the L<small>ORD</small> and do good; dwell in the land and enjoy safe pasture. Take delight in the L<small>ORD</small>, and he will give you the desires of your heart.
—P<small>SALM</small> 37:3–4

The Merriam-Webster Dictionary defines delight as something that gives extreme pleasure. I don't know about you, but my children do not always bring me extreme pleasure. There are many times when they make poor choices, throw temper tantrums, and, to put it simply, are not nice to be around. It can seem counterintuitive to delight in your children when they get under your skin many times throughout the day and make you want to bang your head against a wall. Most days, they are the opposite of delightful. But don't we do the same thing to God? As His children, we are always messing up and not doing what He would like us to do; nevertheless, He still delights us. When we turn our eyes to Him as our Father in Heaven and learn to live our lives for His glory, nothing delights Him more. When we align our lives with what God would have for us, we bring Him immense pleasure. He smiles down upon us with pride swelling in His heart and says, "That's my girl!"

Delighting in your children is not contingent upon their behavior. Delight starts in you. It starts in your own heart and should not depend on whether or not your kiddos are being pleasant. What are the desires of your heart? Do they align with God's desires? God does not delight in you because you are good enough, make a lot of money, or do everything perfectly all the time. No, He delights in you simply because you are His prized creation, and He loves you. His delight is dependent on Himself, not you.

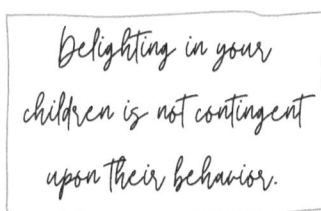

Delighting in your children is not contingent upon their behavior.

It feels easy to delight in the compliant child or the child who doesn't rock the boat. I had no trouble doting over my newborns and babies who didn't talk back or have attitudes and just wanted to be held and snuggled all day—their squishy bodies snug against mine. The immense delight flooded my whole body naturally and with ease. But as these same kiddos get older, more opinionated, and more stubborn, it has become a bit more challenging to truly delight in them. Another mind shift needed to happen for me as I started to parent older children. I needed to zoom out and not focus so much on all the negatives. I needed to realize, as you may need to as well, that we can delight in our children not based on what they do (or don't do) but simply because of who they are: our children. If all you do is focus on the hard or bad, it soon will be all you see. As in much of parenting (and life), when you magnify the positive, you receive more positive; when you magnify the negative, you receive more negative.

> *If all you do is focus on the hard or bad, it soon will be all you see.*

You can delight in your children and your ordinary life, just as Jesus does. When you learn to do even the mundane, ordinary tasks of the day for an Audience of One, God is faithful to fill your heart with delight in the work He has given you. Will you rest in the delight of the Lord today? In the routine, mundane, ordinary tasks of your day, seek to do it all to the glory of your Heavenly Father. True rest for your soul is received when you learn to do as Jesus did, to follow in His footsteps using ordinary, everyday moments to bring glory to God and share His love with those around Him. It is our joy and privilege as mamas to use these everyday moments to share the love of our Creator with not only our little people but with all those looking on. We can rest knowing God uses every moment for a divine purpose—even that pesky laundry.

Questions to Ponder

- ♥ Is there a place in your daily routine where you feel bitterness or resentment growing? Try reminding yourself that God is with you, and He sees you, even in the mundane tasks throughout the day.

- ♥ Read Philippians 2:13–15. Where do you find yourself grumbling in your daily tasks?

- ♥ Where have you seen Jesus in your day today? Where have you been Jesus to someone else in your day today? (Don't overthink it. It can be as simple as wiping a baby's butt. That, too, can be being Jesus in this season of motherhood.)

♥ How do you delight in your children? Do you trust that God also delights in you as His child?

Try This

Try intentionally going on a Jesus hunt with your kids this week. Look for small ways that you see Jesus in your day and small ways to be Jesus to others throughout the day. I promise you will be so blessed, and it will become much easier to find Him the more you practice.

CHAPTER FIVE:
FINDING COMMUNITY

Perfume and incense bring joy to the heart, and the
pleasantness of a friend springs from their heartfelt advice.
Proverbs 27:9

Good friendships and community are vitally important for all
of us, but especially for moms. Healthy friendships provide a
sense of belonging, support, and camaraderie that significantly
impacts our mental health.[14] Research shows that confiding in others
has the greatest impact on the prevention of depression. Compared to
getting more sleep, exercising, or other physical activities, the frequency
of confiding in others (i.e., spending more time with friends you can
confide in) proves miles ahead in preventing and protecting against
depression.[15] If you are in a season of motherhood where you find
yourself feeling isolated and alone, or you're not getting out or seeing
friends often, understand that not only is this detrimental to your ability
to parent well (because I truly do believe it takes a village), but it can also
be very dangerous to your mental health.

My first year of motherhood was one of the loneliest times in my
life. My husband and I got married young and were among the first of
our friends and family to have kids. By no fault of anyone, friendships in
this season began to shift. We found ourselves left out of certain things
because we were the only ones with a baby. Beyond the added stress
and time of starting our family, the rest of our time was consumed by
building our careers—as is the case for most people in their twenties.
During these years, I didn't have many people to lean on to get advice
from or who could understand what I was going through. Although I am
very close with my mother and mother-in-law, I felt a deep longing for

friends—people I could casually meet up with at a playground or grab a cup of coffee with, people I could talk to about the sleepless nights or marriage struggles that sometimes follow having a baby. As much as I adored my son and loved being a mom, the early years of motherhood felt lonelier than ever without any community to share it with.

It wasn't until I put myself out there and started getting more involved at church, including joining a mommy-and-me group that met at the playground once a week, that I could start developing some real mom friendships. I was later invited to join a local Bible study through that group. I didn't know anyone, and I didn't know what to expect, but it turned out to be the biggest blessing in my life at the time. Through that study, I met three of my very best friends who are still in my life today. They are trusted souls I can talk to about anything, who I know will pray for me, encourage me, build me up during life's struggles, and always point me back to truth. I had to put myself out there, take a risk, and feel uncomfortable, but God sweetly brought beautiful friendships into my life in a season when I really needed them.

If you are in a lonely season of motherhood with no community, I encourage you to find your people. Friendship and community lay the foundation for good mental health. It is a hot topic these days but an important one.[16] I am not a psychologist, but I have read enough research and seen enough results in my own life to know that having good friends will truly make or break you in motherhood. We are better together. You were not meant to do this all on your own. Get involved in a mommy-and-me group or join a young moms' Bible study. Find somewhere you can connect with other mamas in the same season you are in. You may have to put yourself out there, try something new, and even feel uncomfortable, but as you do that and continue to pray, God will be faithful to bring people into your circle.

> We are better together. You were not meant to do this all on your own.

As Christian mamas, it is vital to surround yourself with other godly women to do life with—those in the trenches of motherhood with you, as well as those who may be a season or two ahead of you. We need both peers and mentors to have true community. You need both moms who can relate to the daily struggles of your season of motherhood and those who have made it through to the other side. Both offer unique perspectives, encouragement, love, and support that are critical in your mothering journey.

We weren't made to do this alone. God designed us for community and companionship. Throughout scripture, we are often reminded of our need to have others in our circle. God guides us in how to be good friends and choose wise friendships. God did not leave us to figure this out on our own because He knows how important it is to have good, godly people surrounding us to help, guide, encourage, and do life with us. It is essential!

Two are better than one, because they have a good return for their labor: If either of them falls down, one can help the other up. But pity anyone who falls and has no one to help them up.
—ECCLESIASTES 4:9–10

Positive friendships have been linked to increasing your sense of belonging and purpose. They boost your happiness and reduce your stress. Good friendships improve your self-confidence and self-worth, help you cope with life's hardships, and help ease the impact of inevitable difficulties and challenges.[17] We are lonelier than ever, even in a world with all the tools to connect us across oceans and lands. Loneliness seems to be an epidemic plaguing not just our youth but all ages and stages. God reminds us many times throughout scripture of our need for others. True friendships, however, don't take place on a screen. They don't need to be filtered or cropped. True friendships help us see the best in ourselves even when we can't. They encourage us, build us up, challenge us, and maybe, every once in a while, bring us a surprise cup of coffee or a meal when we are just having one of those weeks.

So, how do you find these people? How do you find true, meaningful, positive friendships? Making friends at any age can be intimidating, but it starts with seeking them out. Seek out other moms in your community or your church. If you don't have a home church, I encourage you to find one that you feel comfortable in and that your kids enjoy. Pursue opportunities to get involved in the community or your kid's school.

Putting yourself out there may feel a little uncomfortable, but all of us are in the same boat, and the right people will come along at the right time.

Don't be afraid to be vulnerable and ask for help. True friendships require vulnerability. These friendships are a safe place to show your weaknesses and bring your struggles. True friends do not desire you to be perfect. If anything, I think more and more of us are screaming to know that others are also imperfect and that we are all struggling with something so that we can know we aren't alone.

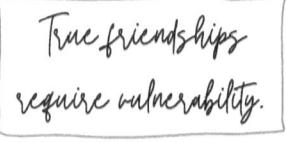

True friendships require vulnerability.

To find friendships like this, we must also be friends like this to others. All relationships are self-sacrificial. We must think of others above ourselves and teach our children the value of valuing others. We preach the golden rule big time in our home: "Treat others how you want to be treated." But how can I expect my children to really understand what that looks like if I am not living it out in my own life? How can you build long-lasting, true friendships if you are not willing to do the hard work of being a good friend yourself? It is not easy. It means sometimes putting aside your own needs or desires, but the benefits of cultivating these types of relationships in your life far outweigh the costs.

Jesus had friends and community. He had many different types of friends—friends with different gifts, challenges, weaknesses, strengths, and abilities. When we watch how Jesus lived with others and implemented rich friendships during His time here on Earth, we can also learn how to do it. Motherhood can feel anything but restful, and it will continue to feel that way if we keep trying to do this all on our own. Let Jesus come alongside you in your motherhood, and let others come alongside you, too—friends who will build you up, see the best in you, and encourage you along the way. Having others by your side will bring rest to your soul and help lighten the load you carry as a mom.

Quality over Quantity

The righteous choose their friends carefully
—Proverbs 12:26

In a social media influencer-crazed world, it feels like the more friends we have, the better. More followers equal more friends, right? This couldn't be further from the truth. Contrary to how social media operates, the quality of friends is more important than quantity. I would even say having one good friend is enough to fill that need. Neuroscientists have studied the effects of social media on our brains and have found that when we get a "like" to our posts, it triggers the same chemical reaction in our brain as gambling or taking recreational drugs.[18] Dopamine, the feel-good hormone in our brain, makes us crave more and more likes. Unfortunately, the more time we spend in this alternative reality, the more depressed and dissatisfied we can become with our own lives.

We need to make sure we are aware of these trends and intentionally build true friendships with real people around us. You don't need a million or fifty or even ten. You only need a small handful of people who are the ones in your corner, cheering you on, who will be with you through thick and thin. Those followers you don't know on social media are not your true friends. True friends will see the best in you, even at your worst. They will set aside time to spend with you. You will feel better about yourself after being in their presence.

It has taken me many years to cultivate my true friends. I do have one friend I've been besties with since we were two. Shoutout to my girl, Britt! Love you, friend! She and I have a rare bond, and she is like a bonus sister. Other than that, I've had to intentionally make an effort with the other friendships in my life. I've had to become okay knowing I am not everyone's person because everyone can't be mine. Many friendships have come and gone in my life; different people have been more involved in certain seasons and less involved in others. Like many other things in life, friendships will have their own seasons. An anonymous poet wrote, "People come into your life for a reason, a season or a lifetime."[19] Wherever you find yourself on the moving scale of friendships, it's most important to know that sometimes they change, which is completely normal and okay.

Nothing is better or worse about these seasons of friendship; they each bring something different to our lives. Proximity seems to be the best indicator of the friendships you have in different seasons of parenting. Those we are closest to naturally become those we spend more time with.

If you don't have people in your life that you see regularly, I strongly encourage you to seek out opportunities to be with others. If you still have babies at home, find a local mom group that meets frequently. Get out of the house! If you have older children, look for opportunities through your church to join a small group or Bible study with other women. Getting involved at your church is one of the best ways to meet people and find other moms in the same boat as you.

You will be so blessed when you take the time to develop good friendships. If you feel stuck, pray for God to bring friends into your life who will help you on the journey. I have found that any time in my life when I pray for God to bring me godly friendships and other women to do life with, He always provides. Don't feel silly asking God for friends. He knows how important it is to be surrounded by those who love and care for you. Sometimes, the people we need the most are already there; we just need help seeing them. Ask God today to open your eyes or open up opportunities to meet other moms and build solid friendships. You don't need many; a few will do just fine. "Psychological research from around the world shows that having social connections is one of the most reliable predictors of a long, healthy, and satisfying life."[20] And this is what God wants for you, my dear friend. He wants you to have a long, healthy, satisfying life with Him and surrounded by others.

> *Ask God today to open your eyes or open up opportunities to meet other moms and build solid friendships.*

Setting Boundaries

As a lifelong people pleaser, I have always found it very hard to say no. I still haven't mastered this skill, but after feeling burned or taken advantage of many times in my adult life, I am learning how healthy it is to say no and set boundaries. Boundaries with friendships aren't something people talk about much. We talk about work boundaries or boundaries in our relationships with our romantic partners, but rarely do we discuss the importance of healthy boundaries within our friendships.

By *boundaries*, I mean *know your people*. Know the people you can let into your inner circle. Who can you trust with your most intimate thoughts, doubts, or fears? Who will celebrate the little things with you? Who would be at your door in a heartbeat if they found out there was a tragedy in your life? These are your people. You can't be everything to everyone; likewise, everyone cannot be everything to you. Only a few people will gain access to your inner circle, not because you don't love others or want to be friends with everyone, but because there is only so much time in the day, and you only have so much capacity.

I'm a bit of a bleeding heart. I am naturally an open and vulnerable person with those around me, but along the way, this has left me feeling insignificant and neglected by others. It has taken me a decade into this parenting thing to really find my people. You will find that friendships, especially in motherhood, come with trial and error. You want to find women with moral and spiritual values similar to those of you and your family. You want to find women who are fun to be around and who don't judge you on the hard days. You need people you can be yourself around. If you have to pretend to be something you are not or always need to feel polished or put together, those are not people who need to be in your inner circle.

I remember a time several years ago when all three of my kiddos were still quite young. I was in the thick of trying to find good friends and would put myself in different social circles. I was invited to a girls' night with a few girls from the church we were attending, women I absolutely adore and love dearly. I was excited and hopeful that I may be invited into their already-established group. Not long into the night, after sharing something vulnerable about what we were walking through with one of my kids, I felt completely rejected and shut down. I know this wasn't the intention, but the cold responses to my struggle instantly made me put up my guard. I remember coming home from that girls' night and sobbing on my bed, feeling defeated and abandoned. I went to bed that evening feeling more alone than before I attended the gathering. I tell you this story because I am still friends with these women today. I still love them and connect with them now and then. But these are not the women in my inner circle.

I've learned to shelter my heart a bit, depending on who I am hanging out with. I am an open book most of the time, and I always want to be real and vulnerable about what I am walking through, especially when it comes to parenting, but I've learned it is not always wise to share everything with everyone. For some, it doesn't come as naturally to love you in the way you need or to respond to your trials in helpful ways. Set boundaries within your friendships, especially with those who seem insensitive to your struggles or leave you feeling bad. However, you may have to experience a few rejections before you find the right people. Not every person in your life will earn the right to know every part of your story. Just like every friend you have cannot be your best friend, not every person you build a relationship with will earn the right to know the deepest parts of your heart.

> *Not every person in your life will earn the right to know every part of your story.*

> *One who has unreliable friends soon comes to ruin,*
> *but there is a friend who sticks closer than a brother.*
> *—PROVERBS 18:24*

Over the years, God has brought me women who speak life and wisdom into my weary heart in the ways I need. I am also able to do the same for them. These are my people. I pray for them, and they pray for me. We know each other's hardest struggles and are real with each other. There is no need to pretend to be strong or have it all together all the time. We can hang out with our five-day dirty hair and workout clothes that most likely have spit up or some smudge from a kid on them. There is no judgment about our cars looking like dumpster fires on the inside or our homes when toys are everywhere. These women love me as I am and help me carry the burdens of motherhood. They bring me encouragement and love me when life is hard. We all need these people.

Community and a sense of belonging are some of the most important parts of motherhood. When you start to build your circle, look for those who lift you up. Who helps make you better? Who challenges you to be a better mom and wife? These are the people you want to surround yourself with when you are in the trenches of motherhood. Choose your inner circle wisely based on your values and the most important things to you in your parenting journey. Find those you can build up and encourage along the way, too, because being a good friend is even better than having great friends. Friendship takes work and intentionality. It also requires trust and knowledge. I recently heard it described this way: you can only trust someone you know, and you can only know someone you spend time with. True friendship requires both. Take the time to get to know other women around you, truly and deeply. It will bless you for the rest of your life to have others in your corner to do life with.

God desires good friendships for you just as much as you do for yourself. Just as He has been faithful in other areas, you can trust He will bring people into your life to surround you and build you up. There will be friends that come for a reason. What can you learn from them? A season, time, or distance will cause you to drift apart. Sometimes, we find those lifelong friends; these are rare gems and should be treated as such. Although it is difficult to make good friends, you can trust and rest knowing that the hard work of searching for your people will pay off. Rest assured, good friends will take time to cultivate; along the way, you may need to set boundaries when searching for the right ones. Good friends offer love, support, encouragement, and sometimes hard truths to help keep us on God's path for our lives. We can find true soul rest as we faithfully cultivate friendships with others who continually point us back to the truth.

BFFs

Walk with the wise and become wise,
for a companion of fools suffers harm.
—*PROVERBS 13:20*

BFFs: best friends forever. If you grew up around the early nineties, you might remember the necklaces, bracelets, and keychains we all used to have with our best friends—a broken heart, usually split in half but sometimes in thirds. Each girl would wear a part of the heart, and when you put the pieces back together, they had the abbreviation BFFs engraved on them, showing the world you were best friends—that is, until you were in middle school and two of you liked the same boy. But I digress.

When you think of your BFF, who comes to mind? Can you think of that person who has been there for you through thick and thin? That person you could call at any time of the night to talk or cry? That person you know you could go on vacation with and who is so much fun to be around? That person who makes your life better just by being in it? Can you think of that person? I have a few very best girlfriends that fit this mold, but have you ever thought of Jesus as your best friend? I know it may sound hard to believe, but think about it—who is a better friend than Him? He is always there with you in both painful and joyful times. He is available to talk any time of the night, and you are never a bother to Him. Just His presence makes me better.

God's desire to fellowship with His creation is woven throughout all scripture. God wants to be our friend and companion. It took me a long time to see God this way. For most of my childhood and adolescence, I saw Him as a rule-maker. In my early adulthood, I saw Him more as a distant father figure who was probably very disappointed in me and wished I would make better choices. After having kids of my own and really diving deeper into scripture, I have come to realize I've had it wrong my whole life. Yes, God is our Creator and Heavenly Father who lovingly gives us rules and boundaries to live by and deserves our complete devotion and praise, but He is also waiting to be our best friend. His main desire is a relationship.

Greater love has no one than this: to lay down one's life for one's friends. You are my friends if you do what I command. I no longer call you servants, because a servant does not know his master's business. Instead, I have called you friends, for everything that I learned from my Father I have made known unto you.
—JOHN 15:13–15

Isn't it amazing that the God of the universe calls you "friend?" It blows my mind every time I think about it. Jesus wants to be your friend, dear one. He wants to walk through life with you as a companion and faithfully show you the way. Advice from your sisters in Christ or your mom tribe is great, but nothing will ever compare to that of Jesus. He never feels burdened by you or your troubles and is the only source that will truly recharge your soul.

When life is overwhelming, and you don't know what to do or who to talk to, you will always have a friend in Jesus. If you feel alone and struggle to find companionship, know that you are never truly alone. You can cry out to Him no matter what or when, and He will hold you in your pain. He listens intently when you pour out your heart longings to Him, and He is trustworthy with every doubt, question, fear, or celebration. Although He may not be able to give you a high five right now or embrace you physically, there is power and peace that comes from spending time with Him and allowing Him into your heart and soul. He is the best friend you will ever have if you allow Him to be.

When life is overwhelming, and you don't know what to do or who to talk to, you will always have a friend in Jesus.

I talk a lot, which is part of what makes me good at being a hairstylist. I can hold conversations for hours while my clients are in my chair. But better than being able to talk is being able to listen. I wouldn't be a very good friend or stylist if all I did was talk. If I monopolized the conversation, it wouldn't leave any room for the other person. Good friends should listen as much as they talk, if not more.

Jesus is the best listener, which is what makes Him the best friend of all. He sees through fake smiles and knows our hearts better than anyone. He is always available, and He isn't screening any calls or texts, thinking, *I'll get to that one later*. No! He is always ready and waiting for you to come to Him. But just as Jesus loves to listen to you, any good friendship must have balance, which means we must also learn to listen. "Take my yoke upon you and learn from me, for I am gentle and humble in heart, and you will find rest for your souls" (Matt. 11:29). Jesus doesn't lay anything heavy on you, my friend. His words bring healing and restoration; His friendship is like honey to your soul.

We all have a deep desire to be truly known and loved. It is imprinted in our hearts and souls from the One who knit us together. I pray that you seek wisdom, counsel, and knowledge as you study God's word and truly seek a relationship with your Creator. He is the only One who knows everything about you and completely loves you perfectly. He is gentle. He is humble. And He leads you as the Good Shepherd to green pastures, giving you true rest and refreshing your soul. (Psalm 23:2-3)

We can find true rest when we give our relationships and friendships to God—when we understand their value and the work they will take-and remember that, inevitably, people are still people. They will mess up and let you down, just like you will mess up and let them down. Don't give up. Rest today knowing that true community takes effort, intentionality, and a whole lot of love and grace.

Questions to Ponder

- ♥ Name a few of your very best friends. If you can't think of any, pray for God to show you who they are or to bring them into your life.

- ♥ Where in your friendships do you need to set up healthy boundaries?

- ♥ What are the most important qualities to you in a best friend? Are you also demonstrating these characteristics in your friendships?

- ♥ How can you spend intentional time with Jesus daily? Find a time or place where you can consistently be alone with Him: in the morning before the kids wake up, during your drive to work, in the shower, etc. Find a consistent, daily time to talk to Jesus and to sit in His presence.

Try This

Think about your closest friends. Send each of them a text letting them know you are thinking about them and asking how you can pray for them. (Bonus: send them a handwritten letter instead of a text.) Nothing is more vulnerable or life-giving than praying for those closest to you. Take time each day to pray for them and allow them to pray for you. Invite them into your story.

PART II

HEALING AND HOPE

*"Come to me, all who are weary and burdened, and I will give you rest.
Take my yoke upon you and learn from me, for I am gentle and humble
in heart, and you will find rest for your sould. For my yoke is easy and
my burden is light."*
Matthew 11:28-30 (NIV)

Are you tired, my friend? Are you weary from the burdens you
carry and the assignment you've been given to raise these kiddos?
You aren't alone. Jesus addresses this very real position we all
come to at some point or another in our lives. The point at which we
can't go on doing what we are doing. The reality is that we need a break.
A real break. A real rest. One that gives us the necessary strength to carry
on and the stamina to persevere through the hard work of raising kids.

I have heard many people say they wish there were one book that
offers everything you need as you go through parenting. There are so
many differing opinions and formulas that, at first glance, you may agree
that there is not just one book that gives you everything you need to
know. We like to cherry-pick advice from many different places, like an
all-you-can-eat buffet. But in recent years, I've come to understand the
opposite. The one book that holds all the answers we need is the Bible.
The Bible is *the* book that teaches us all we need to know, not just for
parenting but for all areas of life. Through parables and proverbs, the Old
Testament and New, God has woven together all the wisdom we need to
live and raise our children well. It is why many refer to it as the Book of
Life. It is the source that leads us to a life of abundance—not a life of
perfection without pain or trouble; we are promised that we *will* have
trouble in this life. Yet God doesn't abandon His people to live this life

aimlessly as we try to figure it out on our own, although we often try to do just that. God is faithful in supplying us with everything we need to know to experience the best life He has for us.

To become the best mom you can be, you must start by stepping into the healing God has for you. You have been called to a life of freedom, joy, and rest, but you must lay down anything holding you in shame, bitterness, resentment, or fear to live within this calling. It is a process to become the mom you are called to be. To step into the true rest that Jesus promises, lay down your burdens. You weren't meant to carry them.

You won't do it perfectly, and you will mess up or fall short along the way, but following Jesus will allow you to rest completely in God's goodness, mercy, and grace. Experiencing true rest in your soul starts with coming to Jesus, learning from Him, and laying down your past while allowing God to heal you in your present. Pressing forward one step at a time, letting His presence and strength be your source of rest.

CHAPTER SIX:

INTIMACY WITH GOD

I seek you with all my heart; do not let me stray from your commands. I have hidden your word in my heart that I might not sin against you.
Psalm 119:10–11

Intimacy is one of those words that we tend to reserve for our relationships with our spouses. We think of it in terms of romantic relationships. Yet the dictionary defines intimacy as close familiarity or friendship and closeness. Who comes to mind if someone asks you about whom you have an intimate relationship with in your life? Most likely, your spouse, maybe your best friend, perhaps even a parent. But have you ever thought of your relationship with Jesus as intimate?

To me, intimacy means that you are close enough to someone that you know them inside and out, and they know you. You aren't afraid to be vulnerable with this person. You don't try to hide anything because you know they love you and do not judge you based on past or current mistakes. They love you and care about you despite your flaws. In fact, your flaws are what make you lovely to this person. They know what you are thinking just by the look on your face.

Having intimacy with God looks different for everyone, but what remains the same is infatuation with His presence and delight in spending time in His word. It's the desire to be with Him constantly as you walk about your day. Just as you

Having intimacy with God looks different for everyone, but what remains the same is infatuation with His presence and delight in spending time in His word.

make an intentional effort to spend time with your spouse or friends, you must make intentional time to spend with God to have a true, intimate relationship with Him. Intimacy with God leads our souls to true rest.

Coffee With Jesus

Very early in the morning while it was still dark, Jesus got up, left the house and went off to a solitary place, where he prayed.
—MARK 1:35

I love coffee! It is one of my favorite foods. I'm don't know if it would be considered food per se, but in my world, it has its own corner of the food pyramid. There is just something about a good cup of coffee that relaxes my whole posture: the smell as it is brewing and those first few warm sips. If you come to my house, a pot of coffee is likely on. I know coffee isn't everybody's thing but hear me out. What I love most about coffee is that it is a means to build relationships. Getting a cup of coffee with a friend could quite honestly be one of my favorite pastimes. And so it is with Jesus and me. We have coffee together every day, and it is my favorite part of the day.

Meeting with Jesus first thing in the morning in recent years has become my favorite part of the day. It gets me in the right head and heart space. His words fill me up so I do not feel I am running on empty before the day begins. Each morning, I set my alarm to wake up before the kids and the hustle of the morning. I make a cup of coffee and settle into my favorite armchair in our family room. I pull out my Bible and a journal, sometimes a study I may be using, perhaps light a candle or drape a blanket over the lamp to soften the light, and I dive into spending intentional, quality time with Jesus. It is our daily coffee date, and I try to never miss one. This time is vital to my emotional and spiritual health. Without it, I am short-tempered, more easily frustrated, and triggered by the everyday happenings of life.

Just as your cell phone needs to be plugged into the correct charger to receive power, your heart needs to be plugged into the proper source to be charged. Mantras, working out, going out, or splurging on other self-care services are great, but they are not the true source. They will not charge your heart or soul properly; they may drain your battery even more if you aren't careful. God is the true source. Jesus knew this and intentionally got up and sought solitary time in the presence of His

Just as your cell phone needs to be plugged into the correct charger to receive power, your heart needs to be plugged into the proper source to be charged.

Father. That same source is available to you and me. When my heart feels overwhelmed in anticipation of the day and in need of rest, spending time with God is the ultimate source of true rest—a rest that satisfies the deepest corners of my heart and gives me the strength for whatever the day holds.

Because I make time daily to plug into the true source, God's presence in my life is real. I can feel His nearness all the time. It calms my heart (which tends to be anxious), gives me the ability to stay rational when my daughter is throwing yet another one of her monstrous fits, and helps me stay composed when things don't go as planned—and they rarely do. I have felt His tender embrace and His compassion recently as I walk through extensive gut and health issues with no clear direction or diagnosis. His Spirit is ever-present with me as I go about my day, and I know I would not feel this if we never spent time together.

Do you crave this? Do you desire to feel God's presence and nearness? Remember that God is the true source. Spending time with Him is the rest your heart desires and needs to carry on at full power. If you never plug yourself into the source, your battery will die before you know it. I challenge you today to set aside daily time to spend with Jesus. We'll get to some more practical ways you can do this later in the chapter but know that spending time plugged into Him as the true source will give your soul life and offer you rest when you feel so desperate for it. It doesn't have to be over a cup of coffee in the morning, but I implore you to find what works for you. Allow Jesus time and space in your day, and He will fill the cup of your heart with something even better than coffee.

Wildflowers

God has a sweet way of knowing all the parts of our hearts. He knows all my deepest, darkest secrets, frustrations, and triggers, as well as all the things that make me smile and bring me joy. I was recently driving down the highway on a trip to Alaska with my oldest son. If you have ever driven in the summertime in Alaska, you know it is breathtaking around every corner. Just driving the scenic stretches of highway is an adventure in itself. On this specific part of the drive, hundreds of thousands of tiny yellow wildflowers were sprinkled all along the side of the road. It was like something out of a painting or a picture book. It felt like it couldn't be real. I remember thinking it was like God had painted them just for me, knowing I would find pleasure in them, knowing they would make me smile.

My relationship with Jesus is my most intimate relationship, apart from my husband. After all, He knew me first. He created every detail He wanted to be just mine: my smile, my personality, my love for gardening and exploring the great outdoors, my sensitive heart, and my desire to impact the world around me. And He has done the same for each of us. He intricately designed *you* to be who you are. You are important. You matter. You are treasured. Just as I felt He gave me those wildflowers to enjoy, He is doing the same for you. What is something you saw today that made you smile and caused joy to bubble up in your heart? Maybe that was something God did just for you.

If you are like most people, it can feel overwhelming to start spending time in God's Word, especially if you are new to it. Maybe you think it is just another thing on your to-do list, so it doesn't become a priority and falls to the end after other things. If you fall into one of those categories, I promise there is no greater investment you will ever make with your time than prioritizing time with Jesus. Even if it doesn't start out feeling genuine, try it anyway. The more you make it a habit, the less it will feel like a chore and the more natural and enjoyable it will become.

You cannot pour from an empty cup. So, what is filling yours? I've had seasons where I felt too busy or tired to add in personal quiet time with God. These have been the most draining seasons of my life and motherhood, where I seemed to be puttering along on fumes. It changed everything for me when I realized it didn't have to be formal; I could meet God in the mess of life. I could sit at the breakfast table for five minutes with the baby in the highchair next to me. I could find little cracks of time throughout the day during naptime or carline. Of course, over time, the more I intentionally sought ways to recharge through spending time in God's Word, the easier it became. It is now more structured into my day, but it didn't start that way.

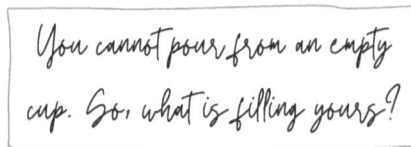

You cannot pour from an empty cup. So, what is filling yours?

Spending time with Jesus doesn't guarantee a happy, care-free life. You will still have struggles, as I do. I still struggle to find contentment, grumble, lose my temper, and fall short every single day. However, spending daily intentional time with Jesus has opened my eyes to His presence all around me, and I continue to see the fruit it brings in my own life. It has grown my dependency on Him to get through life's challenges and my understanding that I can't do this on my own. As mamas, this is what we need most to help us get through this difficult, draining season. More than coffee. More than pedicures or massages. More than running, working out, reading a book, or numbing out in front of a screen. We must plug ourselves into the true source of life, rest, and allow time with God to be our ultimate escape. If Jesus needed time alone with the Father, we can bet our bottom dollar we need it too.

Lonely Places

> *But Jesus often withdrew to lonely places and prayed.*
> —LUKE 5:16

Jesus set a great example throughout scripture by removing himself often and spending intentional time alone in prayer with the Father. He demonstrates that when you are close to God, you can endure hardships that seem beyond comprehension. Thankfully, God will never ask any of us to endure what Jesus did, but He knows that in this life, we will have trouble (John 16:33), so He gives us a perfect example of where to draw our strength when life gets hard.

My mothering journey so far has not been an easy one. Somehow, God decided my husband and I were the parents to handle some of the craziest situations behaviorly with our kids. We've worked hard with them ourselves as well as with outside support from counselors and teachers to help us through different struggles, but to say it hasn't been draining, exhausting, discouraging at times, and isolating would be a lie. For three school years, my oldest struggled nearly every day to go through the gate once we got to school and sometimes to even get out of the car. I remember one incident when he was in the first grade. He refused to go to class once we got to school, so we sat together in the school's front office for almost forty-five minutes, trying to talk to him and calm his uneasiness. Finally, his teacher sent a classmate to the office to help walk him to class. My son went apprehensively. I tried to hold back my frustration and devastation, but I could feel the tears welling up as I walked back to my car. I was emotionally drained by this point and felt overwhelmed with a lot of different emotions.

Going through moments like this made me feel inadequate and alone as a mother. Anyone I talked to about this struggle didn't seem to understand. I felt judged, whether or not people were judging me. I received very little understanding or compassion and even less advice. It was a road of motherhood I was completely unprepared for, and once I was on it, I felt like I was stumbling along all by myself. But this season of parenting was the start of God working on some big changes in my heart. It has been through the hard times that the Lord has drawn me closer to Him. I have learned that I need God for everything and to lean on Him for even the seemingly simple task of dropping kids off at school.

"Jesus often withdrew to lonely places and prayed" (Luke 5:16). Where do you go when you feel lonely? What are you seeking and doing when you are in a lonely place? Maybe you have walked through something similar. Maybe you have been in a situation that has made you feel alone or misunderstood. I want to encourage you today that those lonely places are sometimes the places you most need to be drawn back to God's presence. Sometimes, our loneliness and

> *Sometimes, our loneliness and brokenness are the roads we need to find our way back to Jesus.*

brokenness are the roads we need to find our way back to Jesus. When we feel like we have no one else to lean on, God uses those places to draw us near so that we learn to lean on Him.

Every morning on the way to school, I would pray, *Please, Lord, calm my son's spirit. Please let him get out of the car and go to class today. And if he doesn't, please give me the patience and the wisdom to help him.* A shift began in my heart during this season—a shift to lean on God and praise Him even for the simple things. When my son had a good drop-off, the weight of the world lifted from my shoulders, and I praised Jesus for that simple blessing. We still had plenty of days when he wouldn't get out of the car, but I learned I could trust God even on the hard days because He had been faithful to carry me through them before. As time has passed and this has become less of a struggle, I have seen God working in my heart. As I sit here reflecting on how far we have come from those days, tears flow with gratitude. Although we still deal with our fair share of wild situations, getting out of the car and going to class is no longer one of them.

It blows my mind when I think of how hard of a road that was and how it felt like it would go on forever until one day it was no longer an issue. Life is like that sometimes. When life is dark and things are hard, you feel it will go on forever. But God does eventually lead you out of the wilderness of difficult situations. You may be there for longer than you would like, but it shapes who you are, makes you stronger, and, most importantly, can lead you to lean more on God instead of your own strength and resources.

If you are in a season of motherhood that feels mentally, physically, and spiritually overwhelming, I encourage you to pray. Pray specifically and fervently, and never give up. You may not get an answer immediately, but you can trust that God is listening. You may not even know how to pray or what to pray for. Trust that the Holy Spirit intercedes for you (Rom. 8:26–27). He knows your heart and situation and even cares about the little things you walk through. Do not limit God by your own understanding. Do not let something you feel is embarrassing to go through keep you from bringing it to God. There is nothing too big or too small for God. He cares about it all.

> *Whether you are facing difficult behavior in your child, marriage struggles, family drama, or a dark season that seems to have no end, God's presence is with you and drawing you nearer to Him. Rest in His faithfulness.*

Whatever you face today, if you feel alone, uncertain, or stuck, remember that God is the ultimate source. Plug yourself into Him through prayer and thanksgiving, and He will give you rest—a real rest that can only be found in His presence. Whether you are facing difficult behavior in your child, marriage struggles, family drama, or a dark season that seems to have no end, God's presence is with you and drawing you nearer to Him. Rest in His faithfulness.

Pray About Everything

Do not be anxious about anything, but in every situation, by prayer and petition, with thanksgiving, present your requests to God.
—Philippians 4:6

Motherhood has brought me a newfound love of prayer. Not just for the big things—I find myself constantly and continually praying throughout my day about even the smallest of things. After walking through that tough season with our oldest, I realized how anxious I was every day. I became nervous for every drop-off and every playdate in anticipation of the inevitable challenge. I felt my body tense whenever we went anywhere, anticipating what would most likely happen. It would be a fight to get my son into the car, then another to get him out, no matter where we were going. During this season, I learned to pray for everything and let go of the things I couldn't control.

I still worry about many things as a mom, and I'm sure you do, too. It is what we moms do best—worry. But if we keep this verse close to our hearts, we can be reminded to pray when life gets hard, and that God cares greatly for us. The more time you spend with God throughout your day, the more likely you are to get to a place where prayer is your first line of defense. You will find that God is generous and will give you peace no matter the outcome. Your heart will slowly become more aligned with His will, His purposes, and His plans as you regularly talk to Him.

Now that my children are a little older, I find myself worrying more about bigger things. I worry about who their friends will be, what they are exposed to, who they will become, and if I am giving them all the tools they will need to succeed in life. I worry about the world they are growing up in and the evil we seem to be surrounded by on all sides. For this reason, I keep Philippians 4:6 at the forefront of my mind. It brings my heart peace and comfort in a world that seems chaotic.

You can bring whatever you are worried about to Jesus. He will never blow you off, and He genuinely cares about it all. "Come to me all who are weary and burdened, and I will give you rest" (Matt. 11:28). Are you weary? Do you feel weighed down with burdens that feel too heavy to carry? Jesus is inviting you to come to Him, to walk with Him, and to do as He does. Pray about everything. Bring it all to Him. Let every good, bad, hard, or ugly thing you face be an opportunity to come to Him. Take the burdens you are carrying and lay them down. They weren't meant for you to carry in the first place. Take them to Jesus, and hand them over. Let Him carry the load as you walk this road together. When you do, He promises to exchange the weariness for rest.

Baby Steps

Starting a personal quiet time doesn't have to be complicated. It doesn't have to be a formal thing. If you approach it that way, you will certainly feel discouraged fast. Start simple. Just like our babies started with crawling and moved to standing, shuffling along the furniture, walking, running, jumping, and so forth, we, too, must take baby steps in our faith. You wouldn't take your one-year-old to a track and tell them to run a mile.

In the same way, you must build up spiritual endurance. If you are new to quiet time, this term was burned into my brain from my youth group in the early 2000s. What I mean by quiet time is time intentionally spent in God's Word. The best time for me is in the mornings, but it can be any time of day. I try to wake up before the rest of my house while everything is quiet and still. But maybe you are in the newborn stage of motherhood, and that feels too hard or too demanding. Maybe you work the night shift, so early mornings aren't your thing. That's okay. The biggest thing here is intentionality. If you can remove distractions, great! But, if your home is full of screaming babies and toddlers running around, it may be your season to seek "quiet" time within the chaos.

As the saying goes, don't try to bite off more than you can chew. Start with little nibbles and work your way to bigger bites. Start with five or ten minutes and work from there. It has taken me many years to find my footing in creating consistent quiet time. As I have intentionally carved out this time through the years, it is now easier and honestly the best part of my day. It is my "me" time.

Once you get your footing as you build this time into your routine, try finding a time when there aren't any distractions. I realize not everyone is a morning person, so set a time that works for you. Maybe it is during the kids' naptime in the afternoon, your lunch break at work, or the first part of your evening once the kids are in bed. Pick a time when you feel you will be most fresh and engaged, not a time of the day that is super stressful or when you feel distracted by other things. I've found that if I wait until the end of the day, I am usually too tired and not focused. But this might be the perfect time for you and God to connect if you are a night owl. Whenever you decide to do your quiet time, the most important thing is consistency. Research has shown it takes more than two months before a new behavior becomes automatic—"66 days to be exact." And it can take "anywhere from 18–254 days for people to form a new habit."[21]

The point is, if you aren't already in a consistent habit of having a quiet time, understand it takes your brain time to form the new habit. Give yourself grace, be patient, and don't give up!

Here are some practical and easy ways to be more consistent with your quiet time that I have learned over the years:

- Find a book or study that works through something you struggle with, such as anxiety, prayer, rest, etc.

- Work through a book or a study with a small group or a friend. Having an extra person or two holding you accountable each week can be a great way to start building the habit of spending daily time in God's Word.

- Get yourself a journal and write everything down. I journal my prayers, thoughts, struggles, and praises. When I feel stuck, I find myself looking back on past entries. It helps me see where God has been working and provides much-needed encouragement.

- If you miss a day, don't give up! Pick back up where you left off and keep going. Rome wasn't built in a day. It takes time and intentionality to build up those quiet time muscles.

- Our faith is a journey, not a sprint. Don't rush.

- Be intentional. Set an alarm on your phone as a daily reminder to either dive into God's Word or to sit and pray. I love that my husband has a reminder on his phone that goes off daily at noon to remind him to pray. We can easily get caught up in all our tasks and forget to bring God with us. There is no shame in needing a physical reminder to spend time with God. In fact, I think He would love to know you care so much that you set a special alarm just for Him.

Remember how when you first met your spouse, you wanted to spend every minute of every day with them? Remember how you wished there was more time in the day so that you could keep the conversation going? How hard it was to say goodnight at the end of every date? You just wanted to spend more time with them because you enjoyed being with them. That is how it should be with God, too. When we first become believers and are on fire for God, we soak up every little thing we can get our hands on. We read books, attend services, and listen to worship music in the car. We find ourselves never wanting to be without the presence of God. Yet, over time, we get lax in our time with God, just as we sometimes get lax in our marriages as the years pass.

Just as the longer you are married, the more effort and intentionality it takes to keep the spark alive, we must be intentional and put in the effort

> The more time you spend in God's Word, the more you crave it.

to keep our spiritual relationship with Jesus alive and thriving. Having a daily personal quiet time is a great place to start reigniting the passion you once felt when you first became a believer. As I've seen in my own life, the more time you spend in God's Word, the more you crave it.

Mama, if you are feeling overwhelmed, burned out, and exhausted in this season of motherhood, adding intentional and personal daily time might not feel like a top priority, but I encourage you to make it one. Time with God will fill you up and help sustain you more than you could ever imagine. On many days in motherhood, you can be brought to the end of yourself, in tears, hiding in the laundry room, not knowing what to do next. Yet, spending time with God in His Word and talking to Him through prayer will give you just what you need to persevere and carry on.

When your cup feels empty, remember Jesus is the only source that can truly fill it up. The true rest He promises that you so desperately desire comes from seeking an intimate relationship with Him. Come to Him, spend time with Him, learn from Him, and receive the beautiful gift of true rest.

Questions to Ponder

- ♥ Who in your life do you feel most intimate or vulnerable with?

- ♥ What time of the day do you feel the freshest? Intentionally seek to spend time in God's Word during your freshest moments of the day.

- ♥ Who is the first person you talk to when you feel overwhelmed?

- ♥ Have you ever been in a completely exhausting moment as a mother? Caught off guard with seemingly no one to understand what you were going through? Write down the details of the circumstance and bring it to God. If it is ongoing, pray over it daily and watch Him work.

Try This

Try setting an alarm for a specific time every day for thirty days. Use that time to either read a passage of scripture, journal, or pray. At the end of the thirty days, go back and read what you have journaled and see where God has been working in your daily life.

CHAPTER SEVEN:

HEALING FROM THE PAST

Do you not know? Have you not heard? The Lord is the everlasting
God, the Creator of the ends of the earth. He will not grow tired or
weary, and His understanding no one can fathom. He gives strength to
the weary and increases the power of the weak.
Isaiah 40:28–29

We all bring something different to the table when it comes to motherhood. How we handle situations in our marriages, friendships, and parenting comes from a variety of past experiences, good or bad. You may have grown up in an abusive home or experienced different kinds of physical or emotional abuse in your past. You may have grown up in a seemingly perfect family, and now you feel you can't live up to the expectations and standards of your own upbringing. Wherever you find yourself today, the ideals and standards you hold yourself to are partially a result of where you came from and the experiences you have lived through.

No matter how we were raised or what we have walked through in our pasts, we are all trying to be the best moms we can be. Yet, no matter how hard we try, we are human and *will* fall short. We will fall short of perfection because we can never be perfect. Only Jesus is perfect, and only by spending time with Him, learning His ways, and following His example can we acquire the wisdom and skills necessary to be the best mothers we can be.

There were standards and ideals that I didn't even realize I held myself to as a mother. I discovered these by spending time in counseling processing and unpacking things from my upbringing and past experiences. Counseling is a wonderful tool to help you understand why you are the way you are. I have great parents, and they did their best to raise my siblings and me, but they were not perfect and wouldn't claim to be. I learned a lot about raising my kids from my upbringing, but I have also had to overcome some negative things that I experienced growing up that made me into the person I am.

Unpacking my perfectionism and my desire to control everything was eye-opening. As my counselor and I dove deeper into why I thought I needed to do everything and be good at everything—an unhealthy and unrealistic expectation for myself—it became clear that as a people-pleaser, I put standards on myself to please my parents. I guess we never stop trying to please our parents, even when we are adults. It is natural to want our parents to approve of us, love us, support us, and be proud of us, but it became unhealthy for me when that became the driving factor of my life.

I was a gymnast growing up—a sport constructed around perfection. Every gymnast dreams of getting a 10.0, even though we know it is nearly impossible. However, this mentality crept into my thought life at a young age and has been stalking me ever since. Anything short of perfection felt like a failure. I wanted to be the mom who could work all day, volunteer at school, be at every practice and game, and have freshly baked cookies on the counter when the kids got home from school. The mom who took beautiful vacations, had dinner ready by 5:30 p.m., was never late to any engagement, hosted parties, looked put together, had time to work out and eat healthily, handled every situation with patience and grace, never yelled, and always smiled. The list goes on and on of this *Leave it to Beaver* standard I set for my life. I'm exhausted just looking at that list of who I thought I could be and what I thought was possible. I quickly realized that I was trying to be God. I was so obsessed with trying to be perfect and exhausted from trying to carry the weight on my shoulders that I had put myself on God's throne.

After a lot of counseling and self-work, I had to step back and learn that God is the only perfect One. Our Heavenly Father does not expect us to be perfect. We recognize and appreciate our need for Jesus through our flaws and imperfections. I am so thankful for a God who sees my flaws and loves me anyway. His love is not dependent on following all the rules, being at all the soccer matches, or being involved in all the volunteer opportunities that come your way. His love is not dependent on getting it right all of the time. God's love is not conditional; it is unconditional. This realization

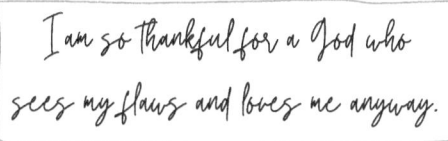

I am so thankful for a God who sees my flaws and loves me anyway.

freed me from so many chains I didn't know were holding me down. Are you also feeling the weight of that today? Do you feel you need to do everything "just so" to be in right standing with God or to be the perfect mom? As my counselor once challenged me, let me challenge you: Who is on the throne?

God's rest is right there for the taking—the rest that seems so far away when you are caught up in guilt, shame, fear, or trying to control everything. When Jesus says, "Come to me . . . learn from me, for I am gentle and humble in heart . . . For my yoke is easy and my burden is light" (Matt. 11:28–30), He is reminding us to come to Him with everything we have—all our baggage, everything that is weighing us down—and to leave it with Him. He invites us to learn from Him and reminds us that He is gentle. If we feel stuck in our pasts, we must let go of our tight grip on them. It might feel safer to hold the past close, but that weight is too much, and you were never meant to carry it. The hard work of processing and overcoming some of the things from your past may be challenging. It may be painful, and there may be a lot of "yuck" you have buried so deeply that it feels better to leave it there, to never talk about it again, but the longer you hold onto it, the heavier it becomes. Jesus' burden is light. His yoke is easy. The healing you need and the rest you crave in your soul can only come from Him.

Mom Guilt

Not only so, but we also glory in our sufferings, because we know that suffering produces perseverance; perseverance, character; and character, hope. And hope does not put us to shame, because God's love has been poured out into our hearts through the Holy Spirit, who has been given to us.
—Romans 5:3–5

Shame, better known to most of us as mom guilt, is a common feeling. I can't tell you how many moms and women I have talked to over the years who struggle with this. Every. Single. One. Whether you work or stay at home, have one kid or seven, sleep train or co-sleep, bottle or breastfeed, homeschool or public school. The list goes on and on. There are so many areas where we feel shame and guilt surrounding motherhood. We never feel like we quite measure up.

So how do we live free from mom guilt? The short answer is grace, but it isn't that simple. Grace is defined as "undeserved favor", "getting what you don't deserve." Our salvation through Jesus is only through God's grace. We also need to learn to accept God's grace when it comes to motherhood. To recognize we won't be perfect and will still mess up. However, God's grace is big enough to cover all our mistakes. You may forget to pick your kid up from school or dance. You may throw away their school project too soon. You may say the wrong thing sometimes. Grace covers it. If God's grace is sufficient for me, it is sufficient for you. You and I have been called out of guilt and shame and into God's overwhelming grace that He showers freely on us as His children.

Positive self-talk has helped me overcome some of my mom guilt moments. How you talk to yourself matters. Do you put yourself down? Or do you forgive yourself when you mess up? Do you talk to yourself like you would talk to a close friend? Or do you tear yourself down? We can be our own worst enemies sometimes, so it is important to talk to ourselves with kindness and grace. Paul writes to "take captive every thought to make it obedient to Christ" in 2 Corinthians 10:5. Our thoughts have power. So often, I let my thoughts conquer me, spinning out of control, allowing them to make me believe lies or hold me captive. But in this verse, Paul is telling *us* to take our thoughts captive: to seize them, trap them, take control of them, and conquer them as an army would conquer a city. What would it look like for you and me to have that kind of power over our thoughts rather than the other way around? We would have much more power to demolish the chains of guilt and be much quicker to remember God's grace and love for us.

How you talk to yourself matters.

Another part of taking our thoughts captive is to make them obedient to Christ, meaning to filter our thoughts through the lens of

Jesus. Donna Burns writes, "The more we think with the mind of Christ and extend His grace towards others [and ourselves] the more we are transformed."[22] Jesus promises us freedom and rest from these negative thoughts when we learn to filter them through His lens.

So how do you do that? How do you stop the lies that try to sneak into your thought life and hold you captive? First, you stop the thought. If you are thinking something negative or outrageous, I challenge you to say it out loud. Ask, "Is what I am thinking true? What would Jesus have to say about this thought I am having?" and then speak truth over them. Jesus said, "I am the way and the truth and the life" (John 14:6) and "You will know the truth, and the truth will set you free" (John 8:32). We'll talk more about this later in the chapter.

Jesus is our truth, our guide, and our light. When the lies start to slip past the strongholds you have placed in your mind, remember to challenge them. Go back to God's Word and speak truth over the lies. When we feel restless in our minds from fighting the guilt, trust that as you bring those worries to Jesus, He will set you free and give you rest.

It takes a lot of work and intentionality to overcome the lies spinning around our thoughts. To overcome shame, doubt, and guilt, we must know the truth of who we are and who God says we are and fill our minds with those things. We must take Paul's advice from 2 Corinthians as well as from Philippians 4:8, which says, "Finally brothers and sisters, whatever is true, whatever is noble, whatever is right, whatever is pure, whatever is lovely, whatever is admirable—if anything is excellent or praiseworthy—think about such things." Don't fill your mind with the lies of the world but with the truth of the gospel. Often, we may feel like failures, but instead of listening to the feelings, we must override them with the truth of who God is and who He says that we are. Some days, you will knock it out of the park; others, you may fall short, but your humanity doesn't define you.

Here are three practices I have used to combat mom guilt:

1. The number one way to combat the lies that creep in, causing guilt and shame, is to speak God's Word, His truth, over them. The enemy will try to twist God's words to tempt you away from the truth and from following God. He did it with Eve in the garden of Eden (Genesis 3) and

with Jesus in the wilderness (Luke 4:1–13), so you can be sure he will try it on you, too. Eve was deceived, but Jesus knew the true meaning of the scriptures, knew God's Word, and used it as His line of defense.

God's Word is a weapon of truth at your disposal at any time and place. Meditating on truth is my first line of defense to combat the lies and guilt that seek to steal the joy of motherhood—the lies that seek to keep me on the hamster wheel of discouragement and discontentment. Let God's words of who you are be the foundation of your own thought life and although you may still have bouts of mom guilt, you will be more quickly able to combat it and step into the freedom and rest God has for you.

> *God's Word is a weapon of Truth at your disposal at any time and place.*

2. The second way to combat lies and mom guilt is through prayer. Prayer is so powerful; it helps you set your mind on things above and refocus and shift your mind to the truth you are seeking to remind yourself of. I love journaling. I know not everyone does, but I find it helpful to write my prayers or journal my thoughts and fears. Something about physically putting it on paper helps me see the lie for what it truly is. In Ephesians 6:18, Paul reminds the Ephesians (and us as well) to pray on all occasions and with all kinds of prayers.

God wants to hear your prayers, my friend. He wants to hear it all, no matter how big or small. You can find true rest and contentment in your motherhood journey and be free from shame and guilt as you seek to pray on all occasions. I pray a lot for others and their struggles and then feel guilty for praying for my own. Don't fall into this trap! You absolutely can and should pray for yourself as well as those around you. Pray that God will free you from any guilt you are feeling. Pray that He will protect you from the lies that always seem to worm their way into your thoughts. Pray about it all and never stop. God wants to do this for you, mama. He does not want you to live in guilt or under worldly pressures. He wants you to live in freedom, grace, and rest.

3. The third thing that has helped me in overcoming mom guilt is accountability. Finding someone I trust to share my struggles with has been irreplaceable in conquering fears, doubts, lies, and guilt. Who can

you share your struggles with? It may be your spouse, a counselor, or a good friend. These great sources can help point you back to the truth of who you are as a child of God—who you are in Him and who He is above it all.

Does mom guilt hold you captive? Do you live your life chained to guilt from past mistakes or wish you could have done something differently? I understand the feeling. But, mama, you aren't

> *Taking our thoughts captive frees our minds from the perpetual lies, and when we give those thoughts over to the truth of Jesus, He kindly offers our minds rest*

meant to live in this captivity. Jesus has broken those chains. He has opened the bars of the shame prison you may be living in. A life following Jesus is perfect freedom. Taking our thoughts captive frees our minds from the perpetual lies, and when we give those thoughts over to the truth of Jesus, He kindly offers our minds rest—true rest from the lies and guilt that plague so many of us.

The Shame of My Past

> *As Scripture says, "Anyone who believes in him will never be put to shame."*
> —ROMANS 10:11

For many years, I struggled with an eating disorder and body image issues. I used starvation and purging to fit the mold of a body I thought was beautiful and "perfect." Did I mention I was a perfectionist? I still deal with the pain of those choices today, and they will forever be a part of my story. However, I refuse to let that part of my story hold any power or shame over me, nor will I let that big part of my life get swept under the rug and forgotten. Looking at that part of my life through a new lens, I can see how God took my shame and transformed it. I now stand on the other side, choosing to stand confidently, knowing that I am treasured, adored, and cherished by my Heavenly Father. I do not need to look a certain way to be beautiful by the world's standards because I now stand on the truth of who God says I am. I am fearfully and wonderfully made (Psalm 139:14). I am seen and known (Psalm 139:2,16). I am forgiven (Romans 8:1), redeemed (Romans 3:23-24), and being transformed (Philippians 3:21). And I am so utterly and completely loved (Romans 8:38-39).

I worked hard for years to heal, to move past my negative associations with food and body image, and to fully understand my true identity as a daughter of God. The biggest transformation is that I don't try to hide this part of my story; I want God to use it. If something I have walked through can help even one person, it is not something to be ashamed of. A big part of my eating disorder stemmed from a lack of identity. Not feeling beautiful in my skin was just an outward expression of my inward struggle to figure out who I was at that time in my life. This was an area where I let Satan deceive me, and yet God called me out. He led me to a place of healing and restoration.

Big lies swirl around your head when you are deep in an eating disorder. Lies that say, "No one will ever know. No one is watching." Lies that claim, "You will never have victory over this." Even the lie that says, "If I just reach this one size, look a certain way, hit a certain goal, I will be happy, and I won't have to do this anymore." Interestingly, something that takes so much self-control ends up controlling you.

It took a lot of time, intentionality, and healing to bring about any revelation in this area. I still have setbacks and tendencies that try to sneak back in, but knowing who I am as a daughter of God, made in His image, is the truth that continues to save me and heal me every day. We, as women, have a lot of pressure on us to look a certain way, act a certain way, and are held to impossible standards of beauty. This is why it is critical to not find your value or identity in anything of this world. Rather, you should look to your Creator to define you. Mama, God shaped you inside and out. You are His masterpiece! Don't let anyone or anything ever let you forget just how beautiful you are.

> Mama, God shaped you inside and out. You are His masterpiece!

I have had to learn to stop the negative thoughts as they come, to take them captive when they do come, and not to give them any foothold in my heart or mind. When they try to sneak in, I remind myself of the truth that my body is amazing. This body of mine helped bring three beautiful babies into the world. It helped feed them when they were infants and held them all hours of the night for years on end. My body is powerful, strong, and beautiful. It isn't about size or weight anymore; it truly is about who made my body and the intentionality that went into every detail. That revelation still brings tears to my eyes; it is overwhelming to think about just how good God is. The truth that God thought about every detail of my body and yours is astonishing. He intentionally gave you every curve, every freckle, and every dimple, and He made you in His image. You hold qualities that the Creator of the universe holds. That is mind-blowing, humbling, and true. These truths hold my heart stronger than the lies about my weight or body image, and I pray they capture your heart, too. I am so grateful for a God who loves us this much.

If you are struggling in the area of body image or identity, please find someone you trust and confide in them. Find a Christian counselor or someone outside your immediate circle to work with. There is no shame in needing help. It takes a lot of hard work and intentionality to forge through addictions and shame like this, but it is possible. You can do it. You can be free if you give it to God, forgive yourself, and move forward in truth.

Maybe you don't struggle with body image but carry some other weight of shame on your back that feels so heavy all the time. Jesus wants you to come to Him. Write down whatever holds your heart so tightly, and then search for verses that will help you speak truth over it. Anytime that lie wiggles back into your mind, take it captive and kill it with truth. God's Word is powerful, and speaking His truth over the lies gives Him authority over them and helps conquer them.

Whatever shame you carry with you today, whether past or present, lay it down. Take that heavy burden that feels too much to bear and bring it to Jesus. Give it to Him, knowing that He will help sustain you. The

> True rest is found in the healing, the releasing, and the grace God freely gives moment by moment.

rest He offers may not immediately remove the pain, but it will remove the shame. Allow Him to free you from shame's chains and walk with you into healing and restoration. True rest is found in the healing, the releasing, and the grace God freely gives moment by moment. The road may feel long and hard, but that weight you feel now will slowly get lighter and lighter.

Anxiety and Panic Attacks

Have you ever been anxious about something? Nervous about how something will go? Felt tense in your body, agitated for seemingly no reason, or troubled by what the day ahead holds? So many women, moms, in particular, struggle with anxiety. The pressure to raise good humans can feel overwhelming, and there is much we worry ourselves with in raising our kiddos. How to discipline them, whether they are eating enough vegetables, school choices, when to have "the talk," how to handle arguments with friends, worries about screen time, alcohol or drugs, and so much more. Moms and dads alike struggle with these worries, but moms seem to carry this weight to the point of letting it cripple us.

If you have ever struggled with anxiety, you know it is no joke. Certain traumatic life events can trigger anxiety or panic attacks, and during the past few years of living through a global pandemic, I think most of us have dealt with our fair share of anxiety and trauma. Sometimes, you can't pinpoint what is causing your anxiety, but for whatever reason, it feels debilitating.

I recently experienced some grueling anxiety. It was so bad I thought I was having a heart attack daily for months on end. My chest was tight all the time, and I felt like a balloon stretched much too big that could pop at any moment. It was terrifying. If you have ever had anxiety, you probably know this feeling. Then, you start having anxiety about your anxiety. I was a wreck of a person during this season, and it eventually led me to make some significant life changes to find healing. Being a people-pleaser and a perfectionist created the perfect storm in my heart, in my head, and physically in my body. I never wanted to say the wrong thing, do the wrong thing, or let anyone down. I wanted to make my clients, as well as my husband and family, happy all the time. It felt like a hamster wheel that I would never conquer and couldn't escape. I never felt good enough, and sadly, it led to a deep depression, making me think that everyone would just be better off without me. I struggled with putting on a brave face day after day, trying to hide the deep darkness that was slowly taking over my whole existence.

I was working too much and pouring into so many people that nothing was left for those I loved most—not to mention nothing for myself. I forgot to protect my mind in this season, and I became crippled by guilt and shame every moment of the day. Being in the beauty industry can sometimes be toxic. Everyone sits down in your chair and dumps their problems on you. Most days, it's not a big deal. It's actually the part of my job I love most—connecting with people. But when you are struggling with your own issues, it can be overwhelming to take on anything else. I often joke that hairstylists are "hair-apists." We do so much more than just hair. I took this role of my job very seriously, but once again, I had started to put myself on God's throne without realizing it, as I had done in my parenting. By trying to take on everything—more than I was ever meant to carry—I felt a weight too heavy to bear.

The straw that broke the camel's back came on a Friday afternoon— the busiest day in a hair salon. I was already struggling to hold my anxiety and depression at bay. I had put on a brave face all day when something was said that broke my spirits. I was with my last client of the day. I got her color on, went to the back room, and fell apart. I sat there and bawled my eyes out. It was the first time I had a full-on panic attack. I could barely breathe, and it took everything in me to go back out, put a brave face on, and finish her appointment. At this moment, I knew I couldn't keep doing what I was doing. I couldn't keep up the charade much longer. My mental health was starting to affect everything around me. Like a cancer that slowly takes over your body, I felt my anxiety oozing into all my relationships. It affected my work, marriage, and, most significantly, my ability to be a present and healthy mama to my babies.

They say that when you are pushed to the limits, it can either make you or break you. Some of us can push through and come out stronger on our own. I had to be broken into a million little pieces before I allowed God to put them back together His way.

Pain insists upon being attended to. God whispers in our consciences, but shouts in our pains. It is His megaphone to rouse a deaf world.[23]

God sometimes speaks to us loudest through the most painful moments in life. We often hear Him more clearly when we feel broken, and I know God used this moment as a catalyst to bring about a big change in my life. We rarely see it in the moment, but when we look back at the pivotal, heartbreaking moments in our life, we tend to see God the most clearly. We see His hand in the details we were too blind to notice during the challenging moments. Reflecting on some of life's hardest moments, I now understand I would not be the person I am today without the difficulties.

> *God sometimes speaks to us loudest through the most painful moments in life.*

Many times in the Bible, we are told about how God removed someone from their familiar, comfortable life and sent them away from all they knew to become who He wanted them to be. God took Joseph away from his family through the painful experience of his brothers selling him as a slave to travelers. He became a servant and a prisoner for nearly thirteen years before rising to one of Egypt's most powerful positions to save a nation from famine (Genesis 37-47). God removed Moses from his cushy life with Pharaoh and the royal family. He became a shepherd for forty years before God called him to lead the Israelite people to freedom from Egyptian slavery (Exodus 2-14). We, too, sometimes need to be removed from our familiar places where we feel comfortable so that God can grow us and equip us for whatever lies ahead.

It took nearly a year after reaching my own breaking point before I listened to God's stirring in my heart, but I eventually stepped away from being a hairstylist for a year to recalibrate. I didn't know what I needed, but I knew God was offering me a life preserver to prevent me from drowning, so I took it. My heart was weary, and I was overburdened. I desperately needed rest, although I didn't know what that meant or what that looked like. I stepped fully into the unknown, trusting God would put the pieces back together. Nothing is more terrifying or freeing than trusting God with the direction of your life. As I leaned into this new season God had for me, I began to feel whole again. I began to feel a healing in my heart and to understand what it meant to rest in God.

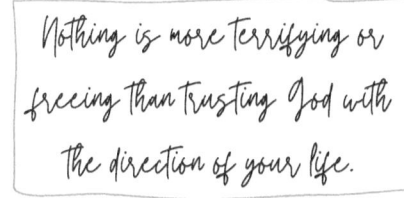

Nothing is more terrifying or freeing than trusting God with the direction of your life.

I didn't stay out of the hair game forever. As it turned out, time, rest, and leaning into new passions and callings God put on my heart during my time away led me back behind the chair, but in a new way. I needed a not-so-gentle reminder that being a hairstylist was not everything and to not put my identity into something that could be gone tomorrow. I have learned to trust wherever God leads because He is faithful and trustworthy and sees the whole picture when I only see one little pixel.

If you are struggling with anxiety or worry, know you aren't alone. One way that has helped me tremendously over the years is to fill my home with uplifting music and scripture. Remind yourself daily of who God is in light of your fears. I keep scripture cards on my office desk, have different encouraging scripture verses painted around our home, and always have my Bible in a convenient place to pick up whenever I need an encouraging word. Installing the Bible app on your phone is also an excellent tool to have God's words at your fingertips wherever you are.

Sometimes fear, anxiety, depression, or panic attacks stem from unresolved trauma or hurt from our pasts. If you have unresolved hurt in your heart, I encourage you to find someone to talk to, especially if these emotions start to paralyze you. A professional Christian counselor is a vital source to offer expert advice, help point you back to the truth of the scriptures and provide you with techniques to fight your worries. Do not let these things drag you down any further. God asks you to "cast all your anxiety on Him because He cares for you" (1 Pet. 5:7). Bring your worries to Him first but know that it is also okay to seek professional help. Sometimes, through proper professional counselors and therapists, God helps you in these circumstances. He cares for you so much, dear one, and wants nothing more than for you to be free from the chains of worry and anxiety in your life. He wants you to walk in freedom from a place of true rest.

Jesus tells us to come to Him when we are weary and burdened, and He will give us rest. Anxiety and fear are genuine emotions; however, when we give them power over us, the weight becomes too burdensome. Anxiety and fear also affect sleep. Are you in desperate need of sleep today? Physical rest can help lead you to a place where you can receive spiritual rest. Have you ever read the story of Elijah in 1 Kings 19? It goes something like this: Elijah, who had been faithfully serving God and testifying against Queen Jezebel's false prophets and gods, was running for his life from the queen, looking for vengeance. He was fearful and beyond tired when he told God he'd had enough and prayed that he would die. Feeling desperate and alone, Elijah cried out to God.

I have been in this desperate place many times. Not always wanting to die, but ready to throw in the towel, nonetheless. Have you been here too, friend? Feeling hopeless and alone, like there was no reason to live? God graciously saw Elijah in his dark place and, knowing what he needed, gave him sweet sleep. When Elijah is woken up by an angel's touch, he is told, "Get up and eat" (1 Kings 19:5). He eats and then lies back down to sleep some more. Again, an angel touches him, saying, "Get up and eat, for the journey is too much for you" (1 Kings 19:7).

> *So he got up and ate and drank. Strengthened by that food,*
> *he traveled forty days and forty nights until he*
> *reached Horeb, the mountain of God.*
> *—1 Kings 19:8*

Elijah was tired. He was burned out. He was weary and perhaps felt abandoned. God saw him and gave him exactly what he needed to continue the journey ahead, knowing it was too much for him on his own. God is doing the same for you and me. Whatever we need, God will provide—sometimes in mysterious ways, but He is faithful to provide exactly what we need. Maybe if you are feeling desperate, you, too, need some sweet sleep and a good meal. Never underestimate the power of being adequately rested

> *Never underestimate the power of being adequately rested and physically nourished and how that affects you spiritually.*

and physically nourished and how that affects you spiritually. It affects your mood and ability to receive true rest in your soul.

True rest brings peace and stillness to a restless mind. Jesus promises this kind of rest. Come to Him. Bring Him every worry, every doubt, every fear, everything weighing you down, and let Him give you true rest for your soul.

The Road to Healing

So do not fear, for I am with you; do not be dismayed, for I am your God. I will strengthen you and help you; I will uphold you with my righteous right hand.
—ISAIAH 41:10

There is a psychology practice called restoration therapy, which has helped me on my road to healing from my past. The main idea is that "insight + deliberate practice = transformation."[24] In layman's terms, restoration therapy teaches you to gain a deeper understanding of yourself and, through intentional and thoughtful repetition, create new patterns of thinking. The four steps of restoration therapy include saying what you feel, saying what you normally do, saying your truth, and saying what you will do differently (and then doing it). You must stand on God's Word to properly move through these steps.

> *Truth isn't relative here. Truth comes from God's Word in the Bible, and we stand on His Truth to fully heal.*

Truth isn't relative here. Truth comes from God's Word in the Bible, and we stand on His truth to fully heal. God is the great healer; Jesus said it Himself in John 14:6: "I am the way and the truth and the life." This foundation is the catalyst for true healing, ultimately leading to true rest.

Using God's lens to help understand your past allows for a different perspective. This perspective uses God's truth to help you overcome unhealthy patterns. In this philosophy, there are pain cycles and peace cycles. Your pain cycle consists of identifying your underlying feelings and coping behaviors.[25] My pain cycle, for example—how I cope with disappointment or failure—is feelings of inadequacy or insignificance. This causes me to feel upset with myself and become negative, which then causes me to react by withdrawing or distancing myself from the situation. This reaction can cause those around me to feel unloved or neglected, then become critical or passive towards me, which starts the whole cycle over again. I'm not proud of how I used to handle situations, but knowing this about myself now has allowed me to work through those tendencies and intentionally make changes to handle things in a healthier way.

The replacement for the pain cycle is called the peace cycle. Your peace cycle consists of identifying your truth (God's truth) and the actions that emanate from that place of truth.[26] In the peace cycle, you learn to cope with situations, disappointments, and failures in a healthier way by inserting the truth about who God says you are and using His truths to fuel how you respond rather than react. For example, instead of coping with disappointment and failure by feeling inadequate or insignificant, I now tell myself the truth that I am significant and loved by God, no matter what. He makes me competent (2 Cor. 3:5), and He never forsakes me (Ps. 94:14). With the reminder of these truths, I am able to respond to the same situations in a healthier way by staying connected instead of withdrawing. Staying grounded in God's truth allows me to stay more connected to those around me.

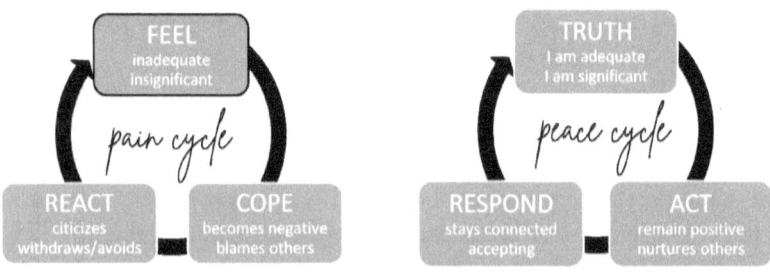

I am not a psychologist or psychotherapist. I am only a mama, just like you, who has worked hard to heal from my past and move forward. It is a daily process, and I have good days and bad days, just like everyone else. However, I know I am happier and healthier mentally and spiritually when I use these tools and this practice to let go of the baggage that has been weighing me down for years. It has helped me forgive more quickly, love more deeply, and be more patient with those around me. I don't feel as stuck in toxic cycles, which has freed me to experience the deepest peace and the ultimate rest that Jesus offers, even in the chaos of life.

The road to healing is not always linear. It is a journey, just like everything in life. You will have seasons of great progress and seasons when you feel stagnant or stuck. I believe if you continue to place God at the center of your life and search for Him amid your struggles, He will bring healing and restoration to your heart. No number of self-help books, podcasts, or self-care days will bring you true healing or true rest. True rest starts in healing and in releasing the weight of burdens. Hand them over to Jesus and allow Him to step into your story—to walk with you and work with you every step of the way.

Questions to Ponder

- ♥ Where is it that you feel familiar or too comfortable? Your job? Your friend groups? Your church?

- ♥ Has there been a time in your life that God has called you out of what seemed familiar into the unknown? Looking back, can you see how God worked and provided in that situation?

- ♥ Is there an area of your life that needs healing? Is there something you are holding onto from your past that you are bringing into your current season of motherhood?

- ♥ Write down the truth of how God sees you as His daughter. Find scriptures that confirm that your identity is found in Him. These can get you started: Jeremiah 1:5, 1 Peter 2:9, 1 John 3:1, Ephesians 1:11.

Try This

Write out some painful experiences from your past that may be holding you back in your current season. Where in your story do you need healing and restoration? Write it out and then give it to God. Ask for His healing so that you may enter the life He has called you to. Look for someone in your circle that you can talk to, whether they are a professional counselor, pastor, or friend—someone who can help you move forward from past hurts and out of potentially unhealthy cycles of behavior.

CHAPTER EIGHT:

FINDING REST

Are you tired? Worn out? Burned out on religion? Come to me. Get away with me and you'll recover your life. I'll show you how to take a real rest. Walk with me and work with me—watch how I do it. Learn the unforced rhythms of grace. I won't lay anything heavy or ill-fitting on you. Keep company with me and you'll learn to live freely and lightly.
MATTHEW *11:28–30,* MSG

It is back-to-school season around here, and my head is spinning as I fill out our calendar for the next few months leading up to the holidays. We have soccer practice and games five days out of our week. We have piano on three days, Awana on one evening, Bible study on two days, and church on Sundays. Throw in open houses, birthday parties, field trips, and upcoming vacations, and I am already overwhelmed before it has even started. I know you can relate. It doesn't matter how many kiddos you have—although the more you have, the harder it is to keep track of the schedule—life is busy, and you are tired!

When we are tired or weary, we seek rest. Rest restores our vigor and gives us the strength to carry on. The word *rest* in these verses originally comes from the Hebrew word *nuakh*, meaning *to abide or rest in*.[27] The rest Jesus is offering means to stop and abide in Him. "Come to me all who are weary and burdened, and I will give you rest" (Matt. 11:28). Jesus is asking us to come to Him, to bring Him the burdens that are weighing us down, and to abide in Him—to let Him be our source of true rest. He tells us to "walk with [Him] and work with [Him]—watch how [He does] it" (Matt. 11:28–30, MSG).

If you study the ministry of Jesus, you see that He was a busy guy. He knows what it means to have a packed schedule. Yet He wasn't burned out and didn't flip out on everyone around Him. Jesus knew His source, the Father, and found His rest there. He beautifully modeled what we should do to experience that same level of rest in our own lives. We see Jesus go off alone repeatedly in scripture. He finds time to be still and quiet in His Father's presence and comes back restored and ready for the next mission. His example is what we should do in our own lives. Yes, taking vacations and having spa days are nice, and removing a few things from the calendar may ease the tension a little, but true rest can only be found in Jesus, the ultimate source of rest.

"Take my yoke upon you and learn from me, for I am gentle and humble in heart, and you will find rest for your souls. For my yoke is easy and my burden is light" (Matt. 11:29–30). I haven't spent much time acquainting myself with farming terminology; however, a yoke is a wooden crosspiece fastened over the necks of two animals, typically oxen, to pull a load.[28] The yoke makes the load easier to bear and allows the animals to work together to accomplish the task at hand. A yoke is also a term meant to represent designation of servitude and the carrying of the burden of a task or mission.

Jesus is asking us to not only come to Him and abide in Him but also to partner with Him and submit ourselves to Him and His ways. My way tends to leave me stressed, spread thin, overwhelmed, and burned out. I typically want to throw my hands up and toss in the towel when I do things my way. Jesus' way brings true rest, comfort, peace, support, and encouragement. His yoke is easy, not because it doesn't press hard on the neck, but because it is lined with love. His burden is light, not because it has no weight, but because it is laid on us with love and is carried together by us in love.

> *Jesus' way brings true rest, comfort, peace, support, and encouragement.*

When we are heavy with the burdens of life, God does not abandon us or leave us to figure it out on our own. If we are brave and humble enough to come to Him, He leads us and refreshes us one step at a time. He gives us true rest as we hand the reins to Him and abide in His love.

Burnout Culture

We live in a burnout culture. We go and go and go until we have a mental breakdown. We overpack our schedules and don't leave much margin for rest in our daily lives. Let's count. How many kids' birthday parties were you invited to last month? How many sports practices or games have you attended just this week? Maybe you are in a slower season, but I'm sure you have been in one of these hectic seasons before. Or maybe it is coming soon. Get ready! Busyness seems to take over our lives, especially for parents, and if we aren't careful, we will burn ourselves out.

With Amazon same-day deliveries, grocery pick-ups, and Uber Eats, there isn't much we have to wait for these days. Just the other day, I ordered my weekly groceries while I was at work and scheduled them to be delivered within minutes of me getting home from my son's soccer practice. This modern way of living does have its perks, especially for those of us who already have too much on our plates. However, with the revolutionary advancements and rush in our conveniences come the implied expectation for us to operate at this speed and capacity, too. Whether you work outside the home or not, the pressure to keep up with the Joneses and continually feel productive weighs heavy on all of us. The assumed mentality is that you are lazy if you aren't pulling in six figures or have a couple of side hustles. This is a recipe for disaster, and we are seeing the results of such thinking in our mental health. Moms are more stressed than ever, and I chalk part of it up to being way too busy.

In this culture of busyness, we must choose rest. "The Sabbath was made for man, not man for the Sabbath" (Mark 2:27). Jesus, the Co-Creator of the universe and mankind, understood the importance of rest. God placed it specifically and purposefully in His plan for us to follow, not ignore. If God chose to rest on the seventh day of creation, we, too, are meant to intentionally seek opportunities and spaces for rest. It is part of our design.

In this culture of busyness, we must choose rest.

R.E.S.T.

I want to make this practical because finding rest does not come easily for me, and I don't think I am alone in this struggle. Implementing these four simple yet practical steps into your daily life can help you find and experience true rest.

R – Remove distractions

E – Entrust God

S – Stay in God's Word

T – Talk to God

REMOVE DISTRACTIONS:

To truly rest, you must first remove the distractions holding you captive. Remove fear, self-doubt, criticism, and any physical distractions. What is distracting you from spending quality, intimate time with God? What is distracting you from spiritual and physical rest in your daily life? Put away the phone. Turn off the TV. Close the computer. Perhaps stay in tonight or dare I say, go to bed early. God is calling you to a life of rest, but you won't hear the invitation if you are too distracted.

ENTRUST GOD

To truly find rest, you must entrust God with your current season or circumstance. Whatever you are walking through today, whether a physical ailment, spiritual battle, or some deep-rooted hurt from your past. You will never experience the true rest God desires to give you until you learn to let go and trust God with it. To "come to [Him]" and allow Him to help carry the weight. Entrusting God is hard. I get it. If you are like me, entrusting God feels scary and like you aren't able to be in control. I like to be in control. Yet, entrusting your heart and burdens to the care of your Heavenly Father, the only One capable of carrying them is the safest place you can be. Allowing God to come alongside you in your pain, frustration, and heartache will ultimately lead you to a place of true rest – spiritual and soul rest.

STAY IN GOD'S WORD

Staying in God's Word anchors your soul to the giver and source of true rest. Nothing else will feed your hungry soul like being in God's Word. The world promises a lot of things, but the level of true rest you

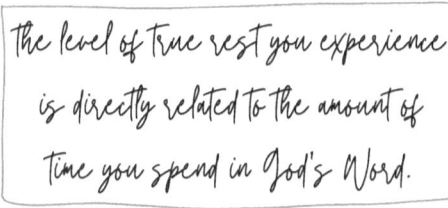

The level of true rest you experience is directly related to the amount of time you spend in God's Word.

experience is directly related to the amount of time you spend in God's Word. The more time you spend in His presence, the more you reflect Him. His words are faithful to bring you hope when you are hopeless, encouragement when you are discouraged, love when you feel worthless, joy when you are full of sorrow, peace amid turmoil, and rest even when the storms of life crash over you.

TALK TO GOD

Talking to God through prayer is a lifeline God freely gives to each of us. It should bring you much comfort to know that you can talk to God at any time of the day or night. I know it does for me. The true rest Jesus offers comes from the Father and from Him. The more time you spend talking with Him, the more you will learn His ways, and the more your heart, soul, and body will be at rest. Prayer unloads the burdens of life and allows you to take on the yoke of Christ. It offers your heart true rest and strength to carry on. True rest is the result of a soul well-connected to the Father.

White Space

There is a term used in art called white space. In painting, it is used to describe the unused spaces on the canvas. White space draws your eye to the elements on the page and creates more interest and elegance in the piece. In other forms of art or design, white space creates separation, legibility, and comprehension and draws the viewers' attention toward a particular element.[29] Some people may look at white space as wasted space, but the artist deems it necessary to create a balance between the different elements. White space makes the page you are reading now legible. Without white space, a piece of art, a photograph, or a novel would be utter chaos.

White space is necessary in art, but this concept is also necessary in our lives. If we fill every minute of every day with something productive, we can easily become overwhelmed and burned out. God designed us to enjoy white space—to enjoy breaks from the tasks of life, allowing for rest and rejuvenation. The seemingly "wasted" time devoted to white space can actually make the remainder of your day feel more productive. Joyous productivity comes when we have a healthy balance of work and rest (I'll add we need fun, too). I find it much more enjoyable to do the dishes, fold the laundry, or clean the house when, every few hours, I pause to do something else—to find some white space.

Recently, I started taking piano lessons. Music has always been a medium that speaks to me, and when I took time off from working at the salon, I wanted to learn something new. I have found that pausing the tasks of my day to sit down and practice piano or play my favorite tunes for twenty or thirty minutes resets my mind to a more positive place where I find myself joyfully doing the housework and other tasks of the day. Breaking up the day's work with little moments of white space helps me get in a better mindset, be more productive, and find more joy, even in the chaos.

White space on a page can also be equated to silence. The value of silence has been lost in our culture today. We turn on the radio in our cars, listen to podcasts or audiobooks while we clean our homes, and have a cooking show or HGTV on in the background while we go about our day. I'm guilty of this, too, friends. I love music. I love listening to podcasts and audiobooks. I love a good demo day. As moms, we are queens of multitasking. I'm not telling you to stop doing that. I also recognize it is vitally important to have moments of your day that are intentionally and purposefully open to silence, to white space. You do not have to fill every second with something productive. God invites us away from the noise of life to walk with Him—to join Him in the white space.

> God invites us away from the noise of life to walk with Him—to join Him in the white space.

By allowing room for white space, we allow room to listen to God's voice. I've learned in my own life that God typically does not speak to me in a booming, loud, domineering voice but rather in a still, small one. —in a whisper, like a gentle breeze. If my life is too noisy or busy, I miss opportunities to connect with Him or hear Him. If you can't hear God's voice in your life, look for opportunities to build in silence and white space.

My kids and I have adopted a new practice over the last few years. I ask them if they want to listen to music or let it be quiet while driving. More times than not, they ask for it to be quiet. This started when my daughter would have enormous fits in the car, and we needed quietness, but it opened up a new appreciation for silence. Don't get me wrong; my kids love music, and sometimes, we have music blaring, but I have noticed something profound in our drives without the extra noise of the radio. The silence frees us to talk to each other. Some of my favorite car ride conversations with my kids have only happened because I have allowed room for silence. I now prefer to leave the radio off when we are all together, and I've even learned to intentionally turn it all off while I'm by myself every now and then and drive in silence - in white space.

As in anything, the key here is finding balance: the balance between white space and content. The balance between busy schedules and lazy days. The balance between noise and silence. White space allows us to experience the presence of God, which ultimately brings us to a state of true rest.

Shalom

Peace I leave with you; my peace I give you. I do not give to you as the world gives. Do not let your hearts be troubled and do not be afraid.
—JOHN 14:27

Shalom. The simple meaning of this Hebrew word is *peace.* You may have heard it used before, but *shalom* goes much deeper than external peace. Shalom encompasses harmony, wholeness, and completeness.[30] It is a word used as a blessing and a

Shalom is an overall sense of fullness and completeness in mind, body, and spirit.

manifestation of divine grace. The ancient meaning of *shalam* (the root word of *shalom*) is *restore*.[31] *Shalom* is an overall sense of fullness and completeness in mind, body, and spirit. During one of the most difficult years of my life, a sweet woman and friend prayed this word over me. She knew I was walking through dark, uncertain times and prayed that I would find inner peace and restoration of my mind, body, and soul. I can't tell you how much this word has changed my life.

Peace goes far beyond the absence of conflict. Peace is something you can have in the middle of conflict. In Paul's letter to the Philippians, he reminds them and us that God's peace surpasses all understanding and will guard our hearts and minds in Christ Jesus (Phil. 4:7). As mamas, most days, it can be hard to find peace. Logically speaking, our days are pure chaos. But that is the point of Jesus. When we go to Him and follow Him, the Prince of Peace, He leads us to true *shalom*.

Shalom is a peace we can have even when our world seems to be falling apart. When we get a not-so-great report from the doctor or a loved one passes away. When our children are experiencing heartache, and we can't do anything to help them. When we feel alone in the shadows of depression or anxiety. God whispers *shalom* over you as His beloved daughter in all those spaces. And His *shalom*, true peace, leads us to true rest.

> *Shalom is a peace we can have even when our world seems to be falling apart.*

> *Now may the God of shalom Himself give you shalom at all times and in every way. The Lord be with you.*
> —2 Thessalonians 3:16, TLV

Do you crave *shalom*? Do you desire true peace in your life? Motherhood is mentally, physically, and spiritually draining, but God promises that when we come to Him and bring Him our burdens, the things that are draining us, He will give us rest. He will restore us from the inside out. He will give us *shalom*.

God does not promise us a life without pain or trouble. On the contrary, Jesus said, "I have told you these things, so that in me you may have peace. In this world you will have trouble. But take heart! I have overcome the world" (John 16:33). *Shalom* is what we are filled with as we learn to trust in the promises of God and as we learn to lean into who He is despite our circumstances. He is good. He is love. He is faithful. He is just. He is strong. He is mighty. He is powerful. He is omnipotent. He is omniscient. He is the King of Kings. He is the Prince of Peace. He is *shalom*. He is our rest.

True rest doesn't mean the absence of doing anything. It isn't being lazy. It isn't a retreat away from life (although it is good to take those occasionally). Rather, true rest is found when we learn to walk with Jesus and follow His example—to quiet the noise around us, remove distractions, seek intentional time with the Father, entrust our circumstances to Him, stay in His Word, and talk to Him through it all. You can find true rest even in the chaos of normal life when you learn to walk with Jesus.

Questions to Ponder

- ♥ Do you ever feel like you should be doing more? When will it ever be enough? There will always be more to do.

- ♥ Where do you go, or what do you do when you feel weary?

- ♥ Where could you build white space or silence into your day?

- ♥ When was the last time you were able to truly rest?

- ♥ Where in your current circumstances do you need to let go and let God fill you with His *shalom* peace?

Try This

Try turning off the car radio or the television during the day when you are with your kids, but also when you are alone. Let a quiet car ride be the catalyst for great conversations with your kids as well as a break from all the noise always bombarding you.

CHAPTER NINE:

HOPE FOR THE JOURNEY

My Lord God,
I have no idea where I am going.
I do not see the road ahead of me.
I cannot know for certain where it will end.
nor do I really know myself,
and the fact that I think I am following your will
does not mean that I am actually doing so.
But I believe that the desire to please you
does in fact please you.
And I hope I have that desire in all that I am doing.
I hope that I will never do anything apart from that desire.

And I know that if I do this you will lead me by the
right road, though I may know nothing about it.
Therefore will I trust you always though
I may seem to be lost and in the shadow of death.

I will not fear, for you are ever with me,
and you will never leave me to face my perils alone.[32]

Thomas Merton

I was so tired during the birth of my first son. After thirty-two hours of labor, little to no sleep in the days leading up to it, and hours of pushing, my body seemed to reach its limit. We had come so far, and I was ready to meet this little guy, but he was having difficulty getting his shoulders past my pelvis. The longer we labored, the harder it became to breathe. The hospital staff put me on oxygen, but the baby's heart rate was not looking good. When it didn't look like he was going to make it, the doctor proceeded to rip him out of me, tearing me from limb to limb. Neither of us should be here today, but here we are. I remember hearing him cry for the first time and then hearing the doctor ask if he was moving his arms and legs. The way she pulled him out could have paralyzed him. Let me tell you, he is a miracle, and he has been a fighter since that first breath.

Gabriel, meaning "strong man of God," has rocked my world since day one. I didn't know where I was going or what I was doing when I first became a mom, and some days I feel just as lost. But one thing remains true: God's faithfulness. As I've watched him grow over the last decade, I can truly say he is living up to his name. Gabe is strong. He is resilient. And he loves God. I know God is going to use him for incredible things one day. And even though I may not be able to see the road ahead or be sure where it will take me, I have hope and assurance grounded in who God is and His unwavering faithfulness through it all.

So much of our lives are filled with pain and sorrow. We experience it every day as moms through complete physical and mental exhaustion brought on by sleepless nights, fussy babies, sick toddlers, and rebellious teenagers. Our hearts ache as we press through each season of motherhood, reminiscing on the past and fearful of the future. Some of us experience children with disabilities, while others experience loss. Our pain in this world is real. Our sorrow is not to be ignored or buried but laid at the feet of Jesus.

> Our sorrow is not to be ignored or buried but laid at the feet of Jesus.

As we learn to let go and give God the authority to write our stories, He is faithful to refine us and create in us something more beautiful than we could ever imagine. God knows your potential. He sees the diamond underneath the surface and is forming you as His priceless creation through the good times and the bad. God may not always remove your pain, but He never leaves you alone in your pain. God's presence is closer than your own breath. If you feel brokenhearted, alone, uncertain, or overwhelmed, there is hope to be found at the foot of the cross. The hope that God offers is more than just a wish for some desired outcome. True hope is an assurance that God will fulfill every promise He has made—

because that is who He is. He is a promise keeper and is with you through it all. Through the uncertainty and the heartache. Through the calm and the storm. Whatever lies before you, today or tomorrow, come to Him, bring it all to Him, and let Him carry the heavy load. Let Him free up your heart and soul to experience the true rest He desperately wants you to have, a rest that brings peace and hope for the journey to come.

Letting Go

When I became a mom, something in me changed. A new person was born that day along with my baby. She was stronger and fiercer. A toughness and a softness arose in my heart that day. I knew I would do anything for that little person. I saw the face of God and His goodness more clearly than ever before the moment I held each of my kids for the first time. Part of becoming a mom meant letting go of who I used to be and embracing the new woman I had become—her new body, sleep patterns, lifestyle, and priorities. It also meant learning to let go of control. Have I mentioned I like control? I don't like change, and I don't like it when things take me by surprise. I wouldn't necessarily call myself a control freak, although my husband may disagree, even if he would never say it out loud. Letting go is hard.

A mother after God's own heart must learn to let go of control and expectations. Not just expectations for herself, but for her kids: expectations that she can do everything; expectations that the house will always be clean; expectations that marriage will stay the same; expectations that it won't be that hard (because it is really hard); expectations that her kid won't ever eat playdough or get in a fight or roll their eyes or say "I hate you!" Motherhood will simultaneously fill you and break you. Yet, this has been one of the most pivotal lessons I've learned in my motherhood journey and what has been the catalyst for finding more joy in it. Laying down my expectations of how I thought this would look has brought me true joy in motherhood and led me to a place of true rest. It has been one of life's greatest teachings.

As you learn to let go of control, you must also learn to have courage, to stand firm in your faith, and to trust. You must learn to take courage when the road feels uncertain and hold tight to the promises of God. As you learn to let go, at the same time, cling to the One who *is* in control,

> When you let go of the tight grip of control you like to hold on to and allow God to lead the way, you can trust that His plans for your life are far greater than you could ever imagine.

the One who holds control. He sees the whole road before you and the end of the story before it even begins. When all you see is the sea, God sees the Promised Land. The same God who led Abraham across many lands, Moses through the Red Sea, and a young shepherd, David, to victory over Goliath is the same God leading you today. He will never lead you astray. When you let go of the tight grip of control you like to hold on to and allow God to lead the way, you can trust that His plans for your life are far greater than you could ever imagine.

"Come to me. Get away with me and you'll recover your life. I'll show you how to take a real rest. Walk with me and work with me—watch how I do it" (Matt. 11:28–30, MSG). Following God in motherhood won't be easy, and you will often question whether you are doing the right thing. But God reminds us to be strong and courageous (Josh. 1:9) because living a life of faith takes great courage and strength. Raising kids takes courage to trust God with the big and small things. Courage to face the hard days and the long nights. Courage to walk into the school meeting with uncertainty or the doctor's office with unclear results. We must trek forward in courage even though we do not see where the road will take us, holding onto true hope that God is with us through it all.

"We have hope as an anchor for the soul, firm and secure. It enters the inner sanctuary behind the curtain" (Heb. 6:19). God's hope is like an anchor. It keeps you upright and steady so that when the waves of life bounce you around, you do not sink. Invite God along for the journey of motherhood with you. Go to Him and walk with Him. It may be dangerous, and you may feel uncertain at times, but He won't leave you alone. He will be your anchor and keep you steady no matter what lies ahead. He promises true hope, lasting peace, and real rest along the way.

Who's the Author?

Something I hear often, especially from the mainstream, is the idea that you are the author of your story. Although it is your life and every choice you make brings about consequences, good or bad, I don't love the self-centered, self-glorifying mentality this presents. Being the author of my story puts me in a place of authority I do not hold. It sounds pretty and encouraging, but in reality, it feels quite daunting. You and I have a choice to hand the pen over to God and give Him the authority that only He should have to write our stories. If we are brave enough to relinquish control, God will be faithful to take every turn and plot twist in your story to develop your character for a greater purpose. Writing your own story may sound great, but what kind of story could you have if you let God write it for you?

> *For God is not the author of confusion,*
> *but of peace, as in all churches of saints.*
> *—1 Corinthians 14:33, KJV*

I've tried many times over the years to write my own story. It never turns out quite as I had hoped. I tried in high school when I dated a horrible guy who treated me like garbage. I thought I didn't deserve any better, so I believed he was as good as it could get. In God's kindness, He wrote an ending to that chapter, and later, when I let go of control, penned a more beautiful marriage than I could have ever imagined to a man who treats me like royalty. I tried again when my kids were little, trying to write beautiful traditions into our lives, but it always seemed to end in chaos. I've learned the hard way to let God be the author and give Him the authority He is due because His story for me is far greater than the one I could ever write myself.

One such occasion was Christmas of 2019. Christmas morning was always my favorite growing up. In anticipation of seeing what Santa had brought, I would hardly sleep and then pop up at the first sign of light to peek over the edge of the banister into the living room. I have carried the magic of that morning with me to this day. I want to create this same sense of wonder in my own home and give my own kids these same lasting experiences. Fast forward to Christmas Eve, the year my daughter turned four. She had dealt with countless ear infections over the course of that year, but they never presented themselves clearly until they were extremely bad. We were getting ready to go to the Christmas

Eve service at our church when my daughter lost it. The only way to describe what was happening is that it was like she was possessed. She was screaming, throwing herself on the floor, kicking, punching, and scratching. Nothing seemed to comfort her. I was blindsided by the sudden calamity. Eventually, we were able to calm her, but ultimately, we decided there was no way we were taking this child into a church full of people, not knowing when the next outburst would happen. So, my husband went on with the boys while I stayed home with my daughter.

Still new to deciphering her ear infections, I wasn't quite sure what to do. She didn't have a fever, and there were no apparent signs that her ears were bothering her, but something was clearly wrong. We changed into jammies and laid on the couch. As I sat tickling her back, my heart sank at having to miss out on one of my favorite evenings of the year. I also feared the next morning. She was so little that it wouldn't matter that it was Christmas. There was a good chance this same thing would happen the next day, although I was praying hard that it wouldn't. It feels silly, but I know a lot of us do it. We work our tails off to create memories and magical moments, only to have them shattered by a toddler meltdown.

Christmas morning came. The boys woke up full of wonder and excitement, but my daughter, not so much. Within the first few minutes, she was already in a full-blown tantrum, and I had a tough time hiding my disappointment. A few days later, we took her to the doctor and discovered she had a bad double ear infection. Because it was her seventh one of the year, this was the catalyst for discussing surgery to get her little ears healthy. One month later, we were in the operating room, getting tubes put in her ears. It was life-changing; she could finally hear better, sleep better, and her little body could work more effectively.

This is life. It doesn't always go as we plan. It isn't like some Hallmark movie where everything gets wrapped up with a pretty bow at the end. Sometimes, plans go awry; we must learn to roll with the punches. We must embrace the story God has given us and let Him be the author. Because although I would have loved to write about a beautiful Christmas morning, my daughter's ears and hearing are clearly more important. Had we not gotten her in for surgery when we did, there could have been extreme consequences. When I feel tempted to take back control, I have to remember God knows best. His ways are higher than our own.

"Come to me." "Watch how I do it." Giving Jesus the pen and letting Him be the true author is another step to finding true rest. So often, I wish I could rewrite parts of my story, erase the heartache, and change the poor choices. But if I could do this, I wouldn't be half the woman I am. If I were the true author of my story, I would eliminate anything uncomfortable and end up being a pretty boring person with a *fine* life. But as my husband says, "Fine is the enemy of good, and good is the enemy of great." We know all good protagonists need to overcome something, but if we're honest, do we like the process of overcoming? Do we like having to walk through the middle of the struggle? Not really. But it is through those moments that God, in His ultimate wisdom, develops us, molds us, and changes us from the inside out. We can rest knowing that God, as the ultimate author, is writing something beautiful. We can trust Him and abide in His omniscience.

There is a beautiful children's book my kids and I love called *It Will Be Okay* by Lysa TerKeurst. It is about a little fox and a little seed who become best friends. The little seed lives in a rickety shed in a seed packet and does not like change. His friend, the fox, is frightened easily and wants to feel safe. The farmer, our God character, plants the little seed in the ground one day. He finds himself in a dark, lonely place, not understanding where he is, and wants to escape. Yet the gardener knows his potential. The farmer knows the seed isn't supposed to stay a seed but grow into a big, strong tree, which eventually provides shade and protection for the little fox. I love this story and wonder how many of us can relate to the little seed. We don't like change. We want to feel comfortable in our familiar environments. It feels safer to stay a seed, yet God sees what we could be. He sees our capabilities and what we really are. It is hard to let go of control and trust God, but you have hope because "the farmer is good and the farmer is kind, and the farmer is always watching over [you]."[33]

No matter what season of life you find yourself in or where your story has taken you so far, there is hope and assurance that come when you relinquish control of your story and trust God with it. God is good, God is kind, and God is always watching over you.

God is good, God is kind, and God is always watching over you.

The rest you crave will come as you lean into who God is molding you to be, even in the uncomfortable, lonely, dark places. He is working. He is writing. He is faithful through it all.

Diamonds

Raising kids can be overwhelming; there can be immense pressure that comes with the job. We do have a big job, mamas! Thankfully, the pressure isn't all on us. The weight isn't all on your shoulders. You do not have to carry it alone because Jesus carries it with you. Your load is lightened when you come to Him and take His yoke upon your shoulders. Your burdens and pressure are lifted. When you feel ill-equipped for the job ahead, remember that God is shaping and raising you, just like you are raising your own kiddos. He isn't done with you yet, mama.

He has made everything beautiful in its time. He has also set eternity in the human heart; yet no one can fathom what God has done from the beginning to the end.
—ECCLESIASTES 3:11

God makes everything beautiful in its time, including you and me. We are a work in progress. We are diamonds being formed in the fires of motherhood and the pressures of life, precious treasures to the King of Kings. Diamonds are a girl's best friend, so they say, and we can appreciate why. They symbolize beauty and elegance and have been prized above all other gems for centuries.[34] Diamonds are created by three things: time, pressure, and heat. For a piece of carbon material to metamorphose into a diamond, it needs both very high temperatures (between 2000-2200 degrees Fahrenheit) and immense pressure (scientists estimate approximately 725,000 pounds per square inch).[35] It is roughly similar to having eighty-six elephants balancing on each other's backs on top of a single dime.[36] In other words, a lot! Do you feel that weight sometimes, too? Like eighty-six elephants are on your back?

Shadrach, Meshach, and Abednego were not spared *from* the fiery furnace. They were spared *in* the fiery furnace (Dan. 3). Daniel was not spared *from* the lions' den. He was spared *in* the lions' den (Dan. 6). We often pray for God to spare us from the fires or the lions' dens of life, but that's where He wants to meet us. Through these hardships, God wants to grow our faith, understanding, and trust in Him. Shadrach, Meshach, and Abednego knew the God whom they served. They trusted Him even if He did not spare them from the blazing

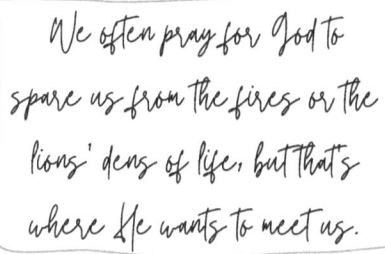

We often pray for God to spare us from the fires or the lions' dens of life, but that's where He wants to meet us.

furnace. Daniel trusted God even if God did not spare him from the mouths of the lions. I want to have faith like that. I want to look in the face of a blazing fire or a lion and say, "Okay, God. Whatever you have for me, let it be. Whatever your will in this situation, I praise you in it."

Just as the diamond is formed under immense pressure, you, too, are being formed into who God has created you to be through the pressures and fires of motherhood. Reach for Jesus in the fire. Go to Him. Learn the unforced rhythms of grace as you walk with Him and allow Him to lighten your load. He is creating something beautiful in you and offers you true rest for your soul as you walk with Him. There is rest to be found even in the fiery furnace.

Your eyes saw my unformed body; all the days ordained for me were written in your book before one of them came to be.
—Psalm 39:16

The majority of diamonds contain microscopic impurities and imperfections known as inclusions.[37] Most are invisible to the naked eye. It is extremely rare to find a diamond with absolutely no inclusions. These diamonds are considered flawless on the clarity scale and have the highest premium. No two diamonds are the same. Even diamonds with the same cut, clarity, and color will not have inclusions in the same places. They are each unique in their own way, a bit like a beauty mark.

This paints a beautiful picture of us as mamas. Not one of us is the same. God has created each of us with different gifts, different struggles, and unique abilities. Just like diamonds, we all contain some inclusions. The only perfect diamond to ever exist among us was Jesus, and because of Jesus, God has placed the same value on all of us, no matter our clarity or imperfections. God doesn't put a grade on you or devalue you because of your imperfections or failures; he already sees you as His perfect child, washed clean and made new. When you are covered with the blood of Jesus, God sees you just as He sees His Son: flawless.

When we learn to see ourselves through the lens of the Father, our souls experience true rest. Your identity and value are not based on what you do or the number of inclusions you have—they are based on the precious blood of Jesus. A flawless diamond is the most beautiful and valuable because of how it reflects the light and sparkles. May we truly live our lives reflecting the glorious God who created us, sparkling and shining His brilliance everywhere we go. May we find true rest and everlasting hope, knowing that even in the fires, even under all the pressure, God is creating something beautiful.

Refined

See, I have refined you, though not as silver;
I have tested you in the furnace of affliction.
—ISAIAH 48:10

There is nothing quite so refining as motherhood. I used to think I was a patient person, and then I had kids. Although we love our children more than life itself, they somehow know how to bring out the worst in us. We get tired and overwhelmed and take out the day's frustrations on the ones we love the most. The flames of motherhood put my seemingly polished and put-together self to the test. I've snapped more times than I would like to admit to my children. I've made my fair share of sly jabs at my husband. The immense pressures of life tend to bring out our true characters: good, bad, or ugly.

Just as precious metals must be refined and purified, we, too, go through this same process. God uses all areas of our lives to refine us, but none feel more relevant than motherhood. Babies refine our selfishness as we give up sleeping for months (maybe years) on end. Your world begins to shift from "me" focused to "them" focused, and slowly, over time, God uses those sweet babies to start a beautiful refining process in your heart. Toddlers refine patience and self-control. Older kids continue the process. And so it goes until our last dying breath.

As God refines you, mama, He is preparing you for the task ahead. What may seem overwhelming today is the exact training and shaping you need to handle what may come down the road. You can trust God and His character even when you can't see where the road

> *What may seem overwhelming today is the exact training and shaping you need to handle what may come down the road.*

is taking you, even when things feel uncomfortable. You can truly rest, knowing that even under pressure, He is working. True rest comes from learning to lean in and trust God in the process of becoming who He has called and created you to be.

Priceless

Where is it that you seek value and admiration? Where do you find your value? Where do you tend to want the most recognition? For a long time, I put my identity in what I did. I thought my various titles in life reflected who I was. My identity was in being a hairstylist, a wife and mother, in keeping up with all the housework or looking a certain way. But in recent years, God has had to work on my heart in this area. I've learned that these are just things I *do,* not who I am. When your identity is in things that you do, the foundation is shaky. Things can be taken away at any moment. When your identity is in those things, you may crumble when they are gone.

Who you are, first and foremost, is a child of God. This is your true identity. "Mom" is a good title but has a wobbly foundation. Who you are is found in the person of Jesus. He is meant to be your foundation because He is unshakeable. "The rain came down, the streams rose, and the winds blew, and beat against that house; yet it did not fall, because it had its foundation on the rock" (Matt. 7:25). Jesus is the rock. He is the foundation. In Him, we find our true identity and true rest.

When I held each of my children for the first time after they were born and looked into their sweet little eyes, I remember feeling completely overwhelmed with love and adoration. I stared at them for hours, mesmerized by their little lips and coos. I didn't have to learn how to love them this way; it came naturally. Did you know that God loves you this same way? He formed you intricately and purposefully to be exactly who you are, and when He looks at you, He sees you as His child—His baby girl. If, in my imperfect humanness, I can love my children in a way that doesn't fade or waver even when they are hard to deal with, how much more does God's perfect love never fade for you and me? This love draws us to the Father. It draws us to Jesus. It gives us the comfort we need when we feel desperate and the rest we need when we are tired.

> *But you are a chosen people, a royal priesthood, a holy nation. God's special possession, that you may declare praises of him who called you out of darkness into his wonderful light.*
> *—1 PETER 2:9*

You, mama, have been chosen for such a time as this. You have been selected specifically to raise those little ones at this exact moment in time, precisely for the children you have. When you feel ill-equipped, let God equip you. When you feel like it is too much, let God sustain you. His presence is the place to seek refuge and find true rest. When the fires of life feel too hot, and the burdens feel too cumbersome, you can always trust God. Your hope and rest are in Him.

> *When you feel ill-equipped, let God equip you. When you feel like it is too much, let God sustain you.*

A Life of Hope

> *"For I know the plans I have for you," declares THE LORD, "plans to prosper you and not to harm you, plans to give you a hope and a future."*
> *—JEREMIAH 29:11*

The Oxford Languages dictionary defines *hope* as "a feeling of expectation and desire for a certain thing to happen. An optimistic state of mind based on an expectation of positive outcomes with respect to events and circumstances in one's life. A feeling of trust." It's a term we seem to use rather flippantly these days. We hope we aren't late for school. We hope our kids get an A on that project they worked so hard on. We hope the dog won't pee on the carpet again. (*Looking at you Pepper-doodle.*) But what is it that gives us true hope? How can we have real hope despite our circumstances, especially regarding motherhood? True hope, as defined in the scriptures, goes hand in hand with faith. "Now faith is confidence in what we hope for and assurance about what we do not see" (Heb. 11:1). Hope takes faith, but not in our own abilities or the outcome of our circumstances. We hope to get a good report from our bloodwork, but our confidence is in a God who is in control even if the report comes back unfavorable. Our hope isn't whether the biopsy comes back clean but in the God who holds us even when it doesn't.

True hope is grounded in the unchanging God of the universe, not our feelings. Feelings are fleeting and can change like the direction of the wind. Feelings change with our circumstances, but when we place our hope in the One who holds all things in His hands, that hope can stand firm. That hope does not get thrown about as our circumstances change but is anchored to the never-changing Maker of the stars. We can still feel disappointed, discouraged, or frustrated when things don't go our way. Our feelings are real. But our feelings only tell one part of the story; they are not the source of our hope. God, being our source, can handle all those feelings. Are you mad today? Are you feeling let down? Are you frustrated? Bring whatever you are feeling to the ultimate source and let Him exchange it for hope.

> True hope is grounded in the unchanging God of the universe, not our feelings.

Your hope isn't in the outcome of your circumstances or other people, not even in yourself. On your own, you will always fall short. Whenever I try to do life on my own, within my own power and strength, I end up more discouraged. To have true hope that doesn't waver when the storms of life crash over you, you must find your hope in something greater than yourself. The only source of true hope is God. When you tether your hope to Him, who He is, and His unwavering character, you find a hope that can withstand whatever life throws at you. That hope brings your soul to a place of true rest, knowing that come what may, there is hope.

I sit here today as a woman and a mom who has walked through some difficult things, although I know I haven't walked through nearly as many hard things as some of you. Some of you have made it through tragedies that make up my worst nightmares, yet we cling to the same God. And we cling to the same hope that come what may, rain or shine, is bound to a Heavenly Father who holds it all in the palm of His hand—a hope that helps us get up every morning and do it all over again, knowing that one day we will see through to the other side.

Mama, motherhood will come with many joys and many sorrows. Many days will leave you feeling utterly overwhelmed and worn out. You will get weary. May God be your source of hope, peace, comfort, and rest in this season of your life. May you continue to pursue His ways, follow His lead, and learn to walk with Him through the journey before you. Don't look for hope in the outcome of your circumstances. Don't look for hope in this world or in other people but in God Himself. *He* is your hope. He is the true giver of hope; it is in that hope that we find real rest—rest for our souls.

Questions to Ponder

- ♥ Have you ever felt hopeless in a situation as a mother? Look back and try to find where God may have been working in that tough situation.

- ♥ Where do you feel God may be asking you to let go of control regarding motherhood? Start praying that God will help loosen your grip on whatever you are holding so tightly.

- ♥ Where is a place you feel God is refining you as a mom?

- ♥ Where do you tend to put your hope or find hope in your everyday life? Is it in God, or do you tend to hope in circumstances or other things? Be honest.

Try This

Think about a time in your life or motherhood journey when you felt hopeless. If you have already made it through, write down all the places God was working in the midst of it. If you are still walking through it, give it to God. Let Him work through it and walk with you in it. Seek out the little blessings even if the pain is still raw.

Writing down past blessings is an amazing way to remind yourself of God's faithfulness for whatever else comes your way. These tangible experiences help strengthen our hope.

CONCLUSION

You made it! Thanks for hanging in until the end. Being a mom is the most demanding, rewarding, exhausting job on the planet. It is a grand adventure requiring daily sacrifice and surrender–surrendering our bodies, our time, and our desires over to God for the good of our children. We sacrifice sleep and trips to the bathroom alone. It is a selfless, sometimes thankless job, but simultaneously fills the heart to the brim. There is no greater challenge and no greater joy.

No matter where you find yourself on this motherhood journey, the days can leave you overwhelmed or lonely. Thankfully, God does not leave you to figure this out alone. He does not abandon you. He promises to never leave you or forsake you. Jesus—Immanuel—literally means "God with us." You can stand on the truth that the God of creation, the King of Kings, will walk with you through every step of the journey ahead.

God sees you in every high and low—in the momentous milestones and the mundane moments that seem unimportant. He is watching over you through it all and promises to shape you over time into something beautiful—to use the good, the bad, and the ugly of motherhood to refine your rough edges and create a masterpiece. To be there with the promise of real rest when you are weary. A true rest that fills your soul even in the chaos of life.

I pray that you carry these truths close to your heart all the days of your life. I pray that you truly and completely understand who you are in Christ: your value as a priceless daughter of the King of Kings and your identity not in who you are as a mom but in who Jesus is. You, mama, have been intricately and purposefully designed to be exactly the mom your kids need. God chose you! You are made enough in Him, and you are capable of raising these tiny humans as you come to Jesus and walk with Him.

"Come to me." Jesus invites you to turn back to Him from whatever you depend on. Bring your hurts, heart longings, fears, and worries to Him. This is an intimate relationship that starts at the foot of the cross. When you come to Him, He trades those heavy burdens for rest, hope, peace, and healing. When your world feels unsettled, turn to Jesus. Go to Him. He is waiting for you with open arms, ready to walk you through this season and all the seasons of your life.

> *The flower doesn't compare itself to the other flowers of the field; it simply turns itself toward the sun and blooms.*

There is no perfect mom. We are each created in the image of God with unique strengths and abilities, and we need each other. We are better together! The flower doesn't compare itself to the other flowers of the field; it simply turns itself toward the sun and blooms. Jesus is the Son. He is the light. He is the ultimate source. Don't compare yourself to others around you; turn towards the Son and bloom right where God has planted you.

Take a deep breath. Pause. Allow God to meet you in the moments of silence and white space. Listen. There is always much to be done. The laundry will still be waiting. Those dishes may be in the sink for a little while longer. The Creator of the universe is calling and waiting for you to come to Him and spend time with Him. There are a lot of things fighting for your attention in this world. Do not be so distracted by the lesser things that you miss God in the moment.

As you make room and space for Him in your life and your heart, He will immensely multiply your time and ability to handle the tasks of the day. He will equip you and shape you into who He wants you to be. God will see to completion what He has faithfully started in you. The journey isn't over, but there is time for rest.

> *The LORD replied, "My Presence will go with you,*
> *and I will give you rest."*
> *—EXODUS 33:14*

Who am I?

Who am I? I am just a nobody from nowhere. A regular mom just like you. Why should you care what I have to say or about my life or stories? Writing this may be one of the scariest things I've ever done—to share bits and pieces of my story with you, complete strangers. Putting very real and vulnerable parts of my life down on paper, in black and white, to be read for all time is daunting.

Yet I am reminded through scripture in stories like those of Moses and King David that we are all just nobodies from nowhere. Moses was a shepherd and an outlaw, yet God used him to rescue a nation. David was a young shepherd brave enough to face a giant, a regular man whom God chose to rule a nation—one who also asked, "Who am I?" (2 Sam. 7:18). And I am just a regular mom from a town you've never heard of making waves in the waters of weary mama hearts. Reminding them that God sees them, is with them, and is waiting to show them what it means to acquire true rest.

God uses unexpected, regular people for purposes only He knows and for things much bigger than we can imagine. God does not call the equipped but equips the called. I am just like you—an ordinary mom just doing her thing, learning the ropes as I go, and trying to raise good kids in this world. What I do know is that you and I have been called to this magnificent challenge of motherhood. It is an honor and a privilege. We aren't meant to do it alone. With community and with God, He makes our paths straight and sees us through to the other side.

If you are tired or worn out today, know I am right there with you. The trenches of motherhood are where God refines us and shapes us into the beautiful sculptures He already knows we will become. May you feel His blessings, peace, joy, and presence washing over you today, dear one. And may you feel encouraged to go to Him, to walk with Him along this journey, and to let Him give you real rest. I am cheering you on and praying for you every step of the way!

SOURCES

1. Sandy Adams, "A Splint and a Flint," SandyAdams.org, accessed December 2, 2023, https://www.sandyadams.org/media/pdf/2405.pdf.

2. Giovanni Papini, "Vita di Michelangelo nella vita del suo tempo" (Milan: 1949), 324.

3. "Am/Em (Mother)," Living Word in 3D, Rock Island Beacon, 2016, https://livingwordin3d.com/discovery/2016/11/07/hebrew-word-study-mother/.

4. Darius Rucker, "It Won't Be Like This For Long," Capitol Nashville Records, track 8 on Learn to Live, 2008.

5. Mark Batterson, Win the Day (Sisters, OR: Multnomah Publishers, 2020), 35.

6. Anne Craig, "Discovery of 'thought worms' opens window to the mind," Queen's Gazette, Queen's University, July 13, 2020, https://www.queensu.ca/gazette/stories/discovery-thought-worms-opens-window-mind.

7. Chaim Bentorah and Laura Bertone, "Hebrew Word Study—Casting Your Burdens," Chaim Bentorah Biblical Hebrew Studies, November 7, 2014, https://www.chaimbentorah.com/2014/11/hebrew-word-study-casting-burdens/.

8. Chaim Bentorah and Laura Bertone, "Hebrew Word Study—Casting Your Burdens," Chaim Bentorah Biblical Hebrew Studies, November 7, 2014, https://www.chaimbentorah.com/2014/11/hebrew-word-study-casting-burdens/.

9. William Temple, "William Temple > Quotes > Quotable Quote," Goodreads, accessed November 25, 2023, https://www.goodreads.com/quotes/7090336-religion-is-what-you-do-with-your-solitude.

10. Ethan Kross, Philippe Verduyne, Emre Demiralp, Jiyoung Park, David Seungjae Lee, Natalie Lin, Holly Shablack, John Jonides, and Oscar Ybarra, "Facebook Use Predicts Declines in Subjective Well-Being in Young Adults," PLOS ONE, 8, no. 8 (2013). https://journals.plos.org/plosone/article?id=10.1371/journal.pone.0069841.

11. Ed Uszynski, "What Does it Mean to Play for an Audience of One?" Athletes in Action, 2023, https://athletesinaction.org/articles/what-does-it-mean-to-play-for-an-audience-of-one-2/.

12. John Ortberg, If You Want to Walk on Water, You've Got to Get Out of the Boat (Nashville, TN: Zondervan, 2014).

13. BTS, "Butterfly," November 2015, track 3 on The Most Beautiful Part of Life Pt. 2, Big Hit Entertainment, streaming.

14. Dr. Brahmanand Nayak, "Is Friendship Good for Mental Health?" DrBrahma.com, July 4, 2023, https://www.drbrahma.com/is-friendship-good-for-mental-health/.

15. Karmel W. Choi et al, "An Exposure-Wide and Mendelian Randomization Approach to Identifying Modifiable Factors for the Prevention of Depression," The American Journal of Psychiatry 177, no. 10 (2020): 944-54.

16. Dr. Brahmanand Nayak, "Is Friendship Good for Mental Health?" DrBrahma.com, July 4, 2023, https://www.drbrahma.com/is-friendship-good-for-mental-health/.

17. Dan Brennan, "Psychological Benefits of Friendship," WebMD, October 25, 2021, https://www.webmd.com/mental-health/psychological-benefits-of-friendship.

18. Jena Hilliard, "Social Media Addiction," Addiction Center, December 7, 2023, https://www.addictioncenter.com/drugs/social-media-addiction/.

19. "Reason, Season, or Lifetime," Poetry.com, June 21, 2021, https://www.poetry.com/poem/103191/reason,-season,-or-lifetime.

20. "The Science of Why Friendships Keep Us Healthy," American Psychological Association, June 1, 2023, https://www.apa.org/monitor/2023/06/cover-story-science-friendship.

21. Kendra Cherry, "How Long Does it Take to Build a Habit?" Verywell Mind, January 5, 2023, https://www.verywellmind.com/how-long-does-it-take-to-build-a-habit-5272517.

22. Donna Burns, "Take Every Thought Captive," SouthFellowship.org, September 25, 2019, https://southfellowship.org/take-every-thought-captive-2-corinthians-103-6/.

23. C.S. Lewis, The Problem of Pain (New York, NY: HarperCollins, 1940) 91.

24. Rhett Smith, "Restoration Therapy: Tools, Resources and Strategies for Working with Anxiety," RhettSmith.com, December 14, 2017, https://rhettsmith.com/2017/12/restoration-therapy-tools-resources-and-strategies-for-working-with-anxiety/.

25. Rhett Smith, "Restoration Therapy: A Concise Road Map and a Simple Tool Leads to Transformation of Anxiety and Depression," RhettSmith.com, May 23, 2018, https://rhettsmith.com/2018/05/restoration-therapy-a-concise-road-map-and-a-simple-tool-leads-to-transformation-of-anxiety-and-depression/.

26. Rhett Smith, "Restoration Therapy: A Concise Road Map and a Simple Tool Leads to Transformation of Anxiety and Depression," RhettSmith.com, May 23, 2018, https://rhettsmith.com/2018/05/restoration-therapy-a-concise-road-map-and-a-simple-tool-leads-to-transformation-of-anxiety-and-depression/.

27. Sarah Fisher, "Nuakh: I Will Give You Rest," Hebrew Word Lessons, April 19, 2020, https://hebrewwordlessons.com/2020/04/19/nuakh-i-will-give-you-rest/.

28. Brannon Deibert, "What Is Yoke in the Bible? Meaning of Jesus' Teaching, Christianity.com, November 10, 2023, https://www.christianity.com/jesus/life-of-jesus/teaching-and-messages/the-yoke-of-jesus-biblical-meaning-and-importance.html.

29. Mads Soegaard, "The Power of White Space in Design," Interaction Design Foundation, September 10, 2020, https://www.interaction-design.org/literature/article/the-power-of-white-space.

30. Susan Perlman, "What Is Shalom: The True Meaning," Inherit, August 27, 2018, https://inheritmag.com/articles/what-is-shalom-the-true-meaning.

31. "Shalom: Peace—Restoring a Relationship with God, Face to Face," Hebrew Word Lessons, December 3, 2017, https://hebrewwordlessons.com/2017/12/03/peace-restoring-a-relationship-with-god-face-to-face/.

32. "The Merton Prayer" from Thoughts in Solitude Copyright Sources 135 © 1956, 1958 by The Abbey of Our Lady of Gethsemani.

33. Lysa TerKeurst, It Will be Okay (Nashville, TN: Tommy Nelson, 2014), 10.

34. "The Value Chain," Petra Diamonds, accessed December 2, 2023, https://www.petradiamonds.com/the-diamond-market/the-value-chain/.

35. Shrutika Srivastava, "How Much Pressure to Make a Diamond?" The Diamond Authority, accessed December 2, 2023, https://www.thediamondauthority.org/how-much-pressure-to-make-a-diamond/.

36. 8448448, "Diamonds Are Created at a Pressure of 725,000 Pounds per Square Inch," Reddit, 2021, https://www.reddit.com/r/NoStupidQuestions/comments/o9r3pf/diamonds_are_created_at_a_pressure_of_725000/?rdt=40258.

37. Brian Boyne, "Diamond Inclusions," Whiteflash, accessed December 2, 2023, https://www.whiteflash.com/diamond-education/diamond-inclusions/.

ACKNOWLEDGMENTS

First, I must thank my supportive husband, who has been with me through every step of this book journey. Thank you for cheering me on, for giving me time and space to write, and for your kind words of encouragement when doubt and fear crept in. You have been a rock in this entire process.

Thank you to my amazing editor, Abby McDonald, who took a very unrefined manuscript and helped polish it to completion. Without your kind words and professional criticism, this would never have come to fruition. I am so honored to have worked by your side through this process.

To Krissy Nelson, Brian Dixon, and all of Hope*Books, this dream would not have been a reality without you. Without your continuous support, guidance, and coaching, this manuscript would still be sitting on my computer, never to see the light of day. I have been completely blown away by the process, but you have held my hand through it all. Thank you for believing in me and in this message.

I also want to recognize my Hope*Books February 2023 cohort. I can't name you all, but every week, I left our meetings feeling uplifted, encouraged, and hopeful that our words matter and that our books are needed. This circle of writers turned friends has been a true lifeline as we all faced fears, doubts, and self-criticism in the writing process.

Last but certainly not least, I must acknowledge *you*: my reader. Thank you for sticking with me until the end. Thank you for reading this book and thank you for supporting a nobody from nowhere. I pray this message resonates with you and assists you in seeking true rest in the chaos of motherhood. You are the bomb, and I am honored to have been your tour guide and partner on this journey.

ABOUT THE AUTHOR

Morgan Ellis is an adventure-loving mother of three, wife to (the other) Morgan, hair stylist, writer, creator, and cheerleader for every mom. She resides in St. Petersburg, Florida, with her family and their wild pup, Pepper. She spends much of her days folding laundry, doing dishes, cooking meals, cleaning the house, and shuffling kids from activity to activity. When she isn't mommin', she is a licensed cosmetologist and still proudly coiffs hair. For fun, she loves to spend time in her garden, have a good cup of coffee with friends, spend time at the beach or in the mountains, play board games with her kids, and, of course, write. Being a mom is her highest calling, and encouraging other moms is her greatest passion.